Best of the World Recipes

Although these recipes have been adapted to healthier alternatives with reduced oil and no animal products, for optimum health it is recommended that you eliminate salt, oil and sugar (SOS) altogether. You will find pencil notations by me where this elimination is easy:

- Substitute a good homemade vegetable broth for oil (or water when sautéing onions and/or vegetables.)
- Substitute apple sauce for oil in baked goods and pesto sauces.
- Substitute Benson's "Table Tasty" for salt.
- Substitute Date Sugar for sweeteners and sugar.

Two of our favorite San Diego Restaurants are:
- *Purple Mint* - all vegan Vietnamese Bistro

- *Jyoti-Bihanga* – vegan neatloaf sandwich, daily vegan specials, soups and bowls.

- Veggie Grill

Love,

Bonnie

The Best in the World II

HEALTHFUL RECIPES FROM EXCLUSIVE
AND OUT-OF-THE-WAY RESTAURANTS

Edited by

Jennifer L. Keller, R.D.

and

Neal D. Barnard, M.D.

ISBN-10: 0-9664081-3-6
ISBN-13: 978-0-9664081-3-3

Third printing, April 2008

10 9 8 7 6 5 4 3

Printed in Canada

Foreword

Back by popular demand, BEST IN THE WORLD II is the much-anticipated follow-up to *Best in the World*—the cookbook for people who adore exotic and distinctive gourmet delicacies. The twist: These cookbooks come with a physician's stamp of approval.

Gathered from restaurants all around the globe, these tasty creations rely on a rich array of vegetables, beans, fruits, and grains, with magical combinations of spice and seasoning, yet they are easy enough for the amateur cook to prepare. Initially selected for their exquisite tastes, these recipes are more than Epicurean delights. They are also among the most healthful foods you'll find anywhere. And where the original recipe may have been a bit too generous with high-fat ingredients, we have made wholesome substitutions. Oils are toned down or eliminated, eggs and butter are replaced by healthy ingredients, and tricks of the trade guide the reader along effortlessly. Many recipes can be prepared in about 30 minutes. The result is a wonderful combination of convenience, creativity, and scrumptious flavor. Whether for an elegant dinner party or a simple lunch for two, dishes such as "Asparagus & Tempeh Salad with Chili Sesame Dressing," "Thai Style Spring Rolls," and "Asparagus Risotto" are sure to become fast favorites.

The original *Best in the World* cookbook was the invention of Neal Barnard, M.D., president of the Physicians Committee for Responsible Medicine (PCRM), a nonprofit organization that has promoted preventive medicine since 1985. PCRM physicians are regularly sought after by major television, radio, and newspaper outlets for their expertise on health and nutrition issues. Through diet and lifestyle habits, in addition to the tools of modern medicine, PCRM doctors empower their patients to play a major role in their own care. The organization stands as the leading authority on diet and wellness, producing unique books, conducting clinical research, and working with government and private organizations to promote good health. *Best in the World* set out to make the journey fun and enjoyable.

BEST IN THE WORLD II was developed by PCRM dietitians, physicians, and writers specializing in the role of nutrition in boosting health and preventing disease. Yet throughout this volume, they have retained the highest standards of taste and elegance.

We owe a special thank you to the chefs and restaurateurs who provided these delicious selections. Thanks also to Neal Barnard, M.D., Stephanie Sarkis, Amanda Stevens, and Harald Ullman. And a final thank you to our talented team of recipe testers: Patricia Bertron, R.D., Suzanne Bobela, Nicole Cardello, Claudia Delman, Jennifer Drone, Laurice Ghougasian, Peggy Hilden, Kristine Kieswer, Kathryn Kuhn, Bonnie Kumer, R.D., Mindy Kursban, Amy Lanou, Ph.D., and Brie Turner-McGrievy, M.S., R.D.

I invite you to experience a world of new flavors and aromas. Dig in and enjoy!

JENNIFER KELLER, R.D.

Contents

Appetizers

HARIYALI KEBABS

Taj Mahal, Lucknow, India

MAKES 12 PATTIES

*T*his restaurant is a haven in this large and dusty city. At Taj Mahal, regional vegetable dishes are served splendidly by turbaned wait staff in a charming restaurant overlooking the gardens.

These tasty kebabs can be served plain or with a peanut or curry dipping sauce of choice, to give them even more flavor.

3 cups cooked yellow lentils	1 teaspoon white or black pepper
2 cups frozen spinach	pinch of salt
1 teaspoon vegetable oil	1 teaspoon garam masala
1 teaspoon cumin seeds	1/2 cup almond flakes or slices
1 tablespoon chopped fresh ginger	
1 green chili, or 1/2 jalapeño pepper, chopped	

Mash the yellow lentils with a fork or potato masher.

Boil the spinach, drain the liquid, and purée in a blender or food processor.

In a heavy-bottomed pan, heat the oil. When hot, add the cumin seeds. When they start crackling, add the spinach purée and cook until most of the water evaporates. Add the mashed lentils, chopped ginger, and chili. Cook for 5-10 minutes over medium heat.

Mix in pepper, salt, and garam masala. Make small, round patties and stuff them with the almond pieces.

Using a non-stick skillet, cook the patties until golden brown. Serve hot.

Per serving: 104 calories; 7 g protein; 13 g carbohydrate; 3.5 g fat; 5.5 g fiber; 73 mg calcium; 30 mg sodium; calories from protein: 24%; calories from carbohydrates: 48%; calories from fats: 28%

CAVIAR D'AUBERGINES

La Bretonnière, Grimaud, France

SERVES 8

ourgonvillia vines cover the ancient walls of this quiet restaurant nestled in a hilltop village above the vineyards of Provence.

6 small eggplants
1 bulb garlic (approximately 10 cloves), with skin

1 tablespoon ~~olive oil~~ *Apple Sauce*
juice of 1 lemon
salt and pepper to taste

Preheat oven to 350°F.

Wash and drain the eggplants. Prick each eggplant several times with a fork and place on a baking sheet.

Wrap the garlic in foil and place the eggplant and garlic in the oven. Bake for about 40 minutes, or until the eggplant and garlic are soft. The garlic should have a golden color.

Remove eggplant and garlic from the oven, remove their skins, and place in a blender. Garlic can be removed from its skin by breaking open the skin and scooping out the soft, cooked garlic. Start to blend and gradually drizzle in the ~~olive oil~~ *apple sauce*. Pour mixture into a medium bowl. With a wooden spoon, mix in the lemon, salt, and pepper.

Serve hot or cold with toasted slices of baguette bread.

Per serving: 129 calories; 4.5 g protein; 27 g carbohydrate; 2.5 g fat; 10 g fiber; 37 mg calcium; 304 mg sodium; calories from protein: 11%; calories from carbohydrates: 76%; calories from fats: 13%

CABBAGE-VEGETABLE STRUDEL

Hotel Gellert, Budapest, Hungary

MAKES 10-12 ROLLS

*H*otel Gellert is home to an ancient natural spring, whose warm waters are reputed to have healing powers. The outdoor patio restaurant, tucked under the steep hills of Budapest, serves health-conscious guests in comfort and elegance.

1 small green cabbage, grated	1 small onion, minced
1/4 teaspoon salt	1/2 cup water
1 teaspoon olive oil	freshly ground black pepper to taste
1 kohlrabi* (turnip cabbage), grated	10-12 sheets of phyllo dough
3 carrots, grated	1 teaspoon soy margarine, melted
2 stalks celery, finely chopped	(optional)

Put the grated cabbage in a bowl and sprinkle with salt. Let sit for 15 minutes. Transfer to a colander and wring out excess liquid. Transfer cabbage to a large skillet, add olive oil and sauté until the cabbage turns a dark yellow color, about 10 minutes.

Add the kohlrabi, carrots, celery, onions, and water. Simmer, stirring frequently, until vegetables are soft and the water has

evaporated. Add freshly ground black pepper. Allow vegetables to cool for 15 minutes.

Fold phyllo sheets in quarters to obtain a rectangle 4 layers thick and about 5- by 8-inches. Place 1/2 cup of the vegetable filling diagonally across the phyllo sheets, fold the short corners over the dough, and roll it towards the long corner to make a log-shaped package.

Place on a greased cookie sheet, loose side down. Brush lightly with melted soy margarine, if desired. Bake at 350°F in the middle of the oven for 20-25 minutes until lightly browned.

When purchasing kohlrabi, look for small bulbs with fresh tops and thin rinds. Large bulbs tend to be tough and woody. Avoid bulbs with blemishes and cracks. To prepare, trim off root ends and vinelike stems. Wash kohlrabi and pare. Cube or cut into 1/4-inch slices.

Per roll: 98 calories; 3 g protein; 18 g carbohydrate; 2 g fat; 3.5 g fiber; 49 mg calcium; 178 mg sodium; calories from protein: 11%; calories from carbohydrates: 70%; calories from fats: 19%

ASIAN GUACAMOLE

Alan Wong's Restaurant, Honolulu, Hawaii

MAKES 4-5 CUPS

The ginger, cilantro, sake, and chili give this guacamole an authentic island flair.

2 avocados, peeled, pitted, and cubed
1 small sweet onion, such as Maui or Vidalia, finely chopped
3 tablespoons fresh lime juice
3 tablespoons sake or rice wine vinegar
1 tablespoon green onion, thinly sliced
1 tablespoon cilantro, minced
1 tablespoon ginger, peeled and grated
1/2 teaspoon Thai chili oil or Thai chili paste

Combine all ingredients in a bowl and mash gently enough to mix, keeping avocados chunky. Serve in a bowl with chips or tortillas.

Per 1/4-cup serving: 40 calories; 1 g protein; 2 g carbohydrate; 3 g fat; 1 g fiber; 4 mg calcium; 3 mg sodium; calories from protein: 3%; calories from carbohydrates: 20%; calories from fats: 75%; calories from alcohol: 2%

STUFFED MUSHROOMS

Gundel, Budapest, Hungary

SERVES 4

*H*ungary's best. After an exquisite dinner enjoyed under the cover of shady trees where a gypsy orchestra plays, visit the little curio shop and stroll in the park across the way.

1 pound fresh champignon or button mushrooms, 1 1/2-inch diameter caps
3 tablespoons soy margarine *or broth*
1 heaping tablespoon yellow onion, chopped
1 heaping tablespoon fresh parsley, chopped
1/8 teaspoon salt

1/8 teaspoon black pepper
4 tablespoons dried breadcrumbs or crushed croutons
2 tablespoons all-purpose flour
1/2 cup dry red wine
1 cup vegetable stock
2 teaspoons cornstarch (mixed with 1-2 tablespoons water)

10

For the filling: Stem the mushrooms. Put aside the 8 nicest caps and chop the rest together with the stems. Place the chopped mushrooms in a colander set on a shallow dish and press the liquid from the mushrooms with a clean cloth. In a small frying pan, melt 1-1/2 tablespoons of ~~soy margarine~~ *broth* over medium-high heat. Add the onion and sauté until golden brown. Add the chopped mushrooms and sauté for 1 minute. Add the parsley, salt, and pepper. Reduce the heat, add the breadcrumbs and flour, and cook for 5 more minutes, stirring constantly. Remove the pan from the heat and let cool for 3-4 minutes.

For the sauce: Boil the wine in a 1/2-quart saucepan until it is reduced by half. Add the vegetable stock and continue boiling until reduced by half again. Season with a pinch of pepper. Stir 1 teaspoon of cornstarch into a little water (a tablespoon or two) in a small cup until smooth and then stir into the sauce. Boil for 3-4 minutes while constantly stirring and then strain through a sieve. Cover and keep warm.

Preheat oven to 350°F.

Cut a thin slice from the top of the reserved mushroom caps so they can sit evenly on a flat surface. Reserve the slices. Turn over the caps and fill with the mushroom filling, using a teaspoon. Cover the filling with the reserved mushroom slices.

In a small frying pan, heat the remaining ~~soy margarine~~ *broth* over medium-high heat. Add the mushrooms to the pan, stuffed side up, and sauté for approximately 3 minutes until the bases turn golden. Carefully remove the mushrooms and place them stuffed side up in a round baking dish, large enough for the mushrooms to fit comfortably.

Bake the stuffed mushrooms until the tops turn slightly brown. Check after 3 minutes. Pour the sauce over the mushrooms and serve hot.

Per serving: 266 calories; 5 g protein; 31 g carbohydrate; 11 g fat; 1 g fiber; 86 mg calcium; 488 mg sodium; calories from protein: 8%; calories from carbohydrates: 47%; calories from fats: 38%; calories from alcohol: 7%

THAI STYLE SPRING ROLLS

Health Haven, Toronto, Canada

MAKES 10 ROLLS

On Toronto's outskirts, this restaurant is dedicated to healthy and delicious cuisine.

10 9-inch rice paper wrappers*
10 soft Bibb lettuce leaves
1 cup shredded carrot
1 cup shredded cucumber

1 cup bean sprouts
1/2 cup chopped, fresh mint
1/2 cup ground, roasted peanuts
  (optional)

SAUCE

pinch of cayenne pepper
2 tablespoons fresh lime juice
1 tablespoon fresh ginger, minced
pinch of sea salt

2 tablespoons sugar
1 tablespoon potato starch (mixed
  with 3/4 cup water)

Soak the rice paper wrappers, one at a time, in warm water for about 30 seconds or until pliable. Arrange in a single layer on a clean, damp tea towel. Place a lettuce leaf on top of the rice sheet and put a small amount of all other ingredients along the center. Fold the left and right sides over by 1-1/2 inches, then fold over the bottom and roll up.

For the sauce: Put all sauce ingredients in a sauce pan and bring to a boil. Cool sauce slightly before serving.

Serve spring rolls cold with sauce. Spring rolls will dry out quickly if they are not served right away. Cover them to keep moist.

* *Rice paper wrappers can be found in Asian food stores. They come in different shapes and sizes and can be used, raw, steamed, baked, or fried. In this recipe, we are using them raw.*

Per roll: 89 calories; 3.5 g protein; 11 g carbohydrate; 4 g fat; 2 g fiber; 32 mg calcium; 83 mg sodium; calories from protein: 14%; calories from carbohydrates: 50%; calories from fats: 36%

Soups

KARTOFFELSUPPE

Rotes Gatter, Lucerne, Switzerland

SERVES 2

*O*verlooking the winding river Reuss in the heart of
Lucerne, Rotes Gatter serves Swiss mountain fare. This
potato soup tastes wonderful, even if you've run out of truffel
oil. We have substituted soymilk and soy yogurt for cream used
in the original recipe.

1 teaspoon peanut oil
1/2 cup chopped white vegetables
　　(celery, onions, leeks, etc.)
1 large potato, peeled and diced
1-1/2 cups water
1 tablespoon vegetable broth paste
3 sprigs fresh thyme, or 1/8 teaspoon
　　dried thyme

5 juniper berries (optional)
2 tablespoons truffel oil (optional)
1 cup soymilk
salt and pepper to taste
soy yogurt (optional)

In a medium saucepan, heat the peanut oil. Add the white vegetables and sauté for 1-2 minutes. Add the potato, water, broth
paste, thyme, juniper berries, and truffel oil. Bring to a boil,
reduce heat, cover, and simmer for about 25 minutes, or until
potatoes are easily pierced with a fork. Remove the thyme and
juniper berries.

Put the soup and soymilk into a blender. Blend until smooth.
Add salt and pepper to taste, blend again, and pour into
bowls.

Garnish with a spoonful of soy yogurt.

*Per serving: 153 calories; 6 g protein; 23 g carbohydrate; 5 g fat; 3 g fiber; 19 mg calcium;
771 mg sodium; calories from protein: 15%; calories from carbohydrates: 55%; calories from
fats: 30%*

BEAN SOUP JOKAI STYLE

Schuch Gourmand, Budapest, Hungary

SERVES 6

The Danube River rolls by this sidewalk café, where you can escape the bustle and size up the lacework on offer from local merchants, all while sipping a bowl of Hungary's traditional hot soup.

2 teaspoons olive oil *broth*
3 cloves garlic, minced
1 large onion, diced
1 cup chopped celery
2 medium parsnips, chopped
2 medium carrots, chopped
2 cans cannelini beans (or other white bean), drained and rinsed

4-1/2 cups vegetable broth*
1 bay leaf
1/2 teaspoon salt
1/4 teaspoon pepper
1/2 teaspoon liquid smoke
1 cup chopped vegetarian Canadian bacon (optional) *or Facon bacon*

Heat the olive oil *broth* in a non-stick Dutch oven over medium-high heat. Add the garlic, onion, and celery, cooking until softened. Add the parsnips and carrots. Cook until softened, adding vegetable broth to prevent sticking. Add the remaining ingredients and simmer for 10 minutes.

Serve with crusty bread or a fruit salad.

* *For a lower sodium soup, replace some or all of the vegetable broth with water.*

Per serving (with vegetarian bacon): 267 calories; 10.5 g protein; 37 g carbohydrate; 10 g fat; 9 g fiber; 85 mg calcium; 1402 mg sodium; calories from protein: 14%; calories from carbohydrates: 54%; calories from fats: 32%

Per serving (without vegetarian bacon): 193 calories; 8 g protein; 36 g carbohydrate; 3 g fat; 8.5 g fiber; 80 mg calcium; 1051 mg sodium; calories from protein: 15%; calories from carbohydrates: 72%; calories from fats: 13%

GEMÜSESUPPE

Griechenbeisl, Vienna, Austria

SERVES 4

*B*eethoven and Mozart ate here. So did Mark Twain. Since 1450, this cozy restaurant with wood-paneled walls has served traditional Austrian food, with some excellent recent adjustments for health-conscious patrons. This vegetable soup calls for kohlrabi, another name for turnip cabbage. The flavor of its bulb-like stem is similar to a turnip.

2 teaspoons sesame or vegetable oil *broth*
1/2 medium yellow onion, chopped
2 cloves garlic, chopped
1 cup chopped yellow turnips
1 cup chopped carrots
1 cup chopped celery
2 cups chopped cauliflower florets
1 cup pared and cubed kohlrabi*
1 cup green peas

3 tablespoons flour
48 fluid ounces vegetable stock, or
    32 fluid ounces for a thicker soup
1 cup dried chanterelle mushrooms,
    or 2 cups fresh, chopped chant-
    erelle mushrooms
1/2 teaspoon marjoram
salt and pepper to taste
chopped parsley (garnish)

Sauté chopped onions in oil in a large skillet until lightly brown. Add chopped garlic. Add chopped vegetables and peas and sprinkle with a light coating of flour. Simmer for several minutes. Transfer to a large pot, add the vegetable stock, and cook until vegetables are tender. Add the mushrooms, marjoram, salt, and pepper.

Decorate with chopped parsley to serve.

* For purchasing tips, please see page 9, Cabbage-Vegetable Strudel recipe.

Per serving: 168 calories; 10 g protein; 28 g carbohydrate; 4 g fat; 8 g fiber; 79 mg calcium; 1285 mg sodium; calories from protein: 21%; calories from carbohydrates: 61%; calories from fats: 18%

SOUPE AU PISTOU

Le Rive Droit, Nice, France

SERVES 6

*J*ust across from the modern art museum in old Nice, locals argue politics in the bar attached to this intimate restaurant serving authentic Niçoise cuisine. *Pistou* is Niçoise for pesto, a sumptuous basil paste. Using vegan parmesan cheese or nutritional yeast instead of aged cheese in the pistou lessens the fat and cholesterol content.

SOUP

1 leek, chopped
1/2 medium yellow onion, chopped
3 cloves garlic, minced
1 tablespoon olive oil *broth*
2 smoked soy sausages, cut into pieces
4 cups water
1 medium potato, chopped into small chunks

1 medium turnip, chopped into small chunks
4 medium carrots, chopped into coins
3 stalks celery, chopped
1 cup chopped green beans
1 medium zucchini, sliced
1 cup pasta (uncooked)

PISTOU

1 clove garlic
15 leaves fresh basil
1/8 teaspoon salt
1/8 teaspoon pepper

1 tablespoon vegan parmesan cheese or nutritional yeast
1 tablespoon olive oil *broth*

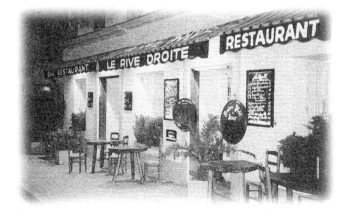

Sauté the leek, onion, and garlic in 1 tablespoon olive oil for 5 minutes. Set aside.

Put the soy sausage in 4 cups of water and cook for 30 minutes. Add the leek mixture and then the vegetables in the order above, and let simmer for another 45 minutes. Then add the uncooked pasta and continue to cook until pasta is tender.

Meanwhile, prepare the pistou. In a mixer, blend the garlic clove, basil, salt, pepper, vegan parmesan cheese, and olive oil.

Before serving, add a tablespoon of pistou to each bowl of soup and mix in.

Per serving: 183 calories; 6 g protein; 26 g carbohydrate; 7 g fat; 5 g fiber; 67 mg calcium; 218 mg sodium; calories from protein: 13%; calories from carbohydrates: 53%; calories from fats: 34%

LENTIL SOUP

Stage Door Deli Café, New York, New York

SERVES 6

his fast-lane deli on Broadway in New York City supplies a wealth of homemade breads, cakes, and soups daily, including this mouth-watering, belly-warming lentil soup.

1/4 cup olive oil ~~broth~~	6-8 cups of water
3 onions, coarsely chopped	1 large bay leaf
2 cups rinsed, dried lentils	salt and freshly ground pepper to taste
2 medium carrots, scraped and chopped	1/4 cup wine vinegar
3 garlic cloves, finely chopped	1 whole boiled potato, mashed, to be added at the end for more thickness (optional)
1 15-ounce can of tomato sauce	
2 tablespoons fresh oregano, chopped	

In a large soup pot, combine all the ingredients except for the wine vinegar and potato. Cover, bring to a boil, reduce heat to low, and simmer for 60-90 minutes, or until lentils are very tender. Add more water if necessary. Before removing from heat, add the wine vinegar and, if desired, the mashed potato.

Per serving: 354 calories; 20 g protein; 50 g carbohydrate; 10 g fat; 22 g fiber; 64 mg calcium; 447 mg sodium; calories from protein: 22%; calories from carbohydrates: 54%; calories from fats: 24%

Grilled Vegetable Gazpacho

The Lanesborough, London, England

SERVES 4

*S*erved as is, this soup has a rustic, smoky flavor. For a milder taste, stir in a spoonful of eggless mayonnaise.

12 ounces plum tomatoes, ripe but firm
1 red pepper, halved and deseeded
1 green pepper, halved and deseeded
1 small red onion, cut in 1/4-inch rings
6 tablespoons ~~olive oil~~* broth
2 slices white bread, soaked in water for 10 minutes, then squeezed out
1/2 cucumber, chopped
2 cloves garlic

2 tablespoons red wine vinegar
2 cups water
1 tablespoon fresh oregano leaves
4 fresh basil leaves, plus extra to garnish
1/2 teaspoon ground cumin
1/2 teaspoon granulated sugar
3 tablespoons tomato ketchup**
salt and freshly ground pepper to taste
croutons (garnish)

Brush the tomatoes, peppers, and onion with 2 tablespoons of olive oil. Grill the vegetables on a hot grill for 10 minutes, turning occasionally until lightly charred all over; let cool.

Once cool, remove the skins and finely dice the vegetables. Place in a large bowl reserving 2 tablespoons of the diced vegetables. Crumble the squeezed bread into the bowl, then add the cucumber, garlic, vinegar, water, herbs, cumin, and remaining 4 tablespoons of oil. Add the sugar and ketchup and leave in the refrigerator to marinate for at least 6 hours.

Blend to a fine purée in a blender or food processor. Strain through a coarse strainer. Serve well chilled, in individual bowls, with the reserved vegetables, salt and pepper as needed, and a few croutons sprinkled on top.

Garnish with basil leaves.

*For a lower fat gazpacho, use only 2 tablespoons of oil in the marinade.

**Ketchup adds an extra sweetness, but you can substitute a tablespoon of tomato purée if you prefer.

Per serving: 283 calories; 3 g protein; 22 g carbohydrate; 21 g fat; 3 g fiber; 41 mg calcium; 228 mg sodium; calories from protein: 5%; calories from carbohydrates: 30%; calories from fats: 65%

CHILLED SORREL SOUP

The Painted Table, Seattle, Washington

SERVES 4

This sunny restaurant in a renowned Seattle hotel serves some of the most unusual cuisine in the Pacific Northwest. Sorrel is a perennial found in pastures throughout Europe and is grown for its leaves, which are used fresh in salads and soups or prepared like spinach or cabbage.

1 bulb garlic, roasted
2-1/2 teaspoons ~~olive oil~~ broth
1 onion, finely diced
1 carrot, finely diced
1 stalk celery, finely diced

1 potato, peeled and diced
6 cups vegetable stock
1/2 pound sorrel, coarsely chopped
salt and white pepper to taste

Preheat oven to 350°F.

Remove some of the excess parchment-like skin from the outside of the garlic bulb. Slice off the top of the bulb, exposing the individual garlic cloves. Drizzle 1/2 teaspoon of ~~olive oil~~ broth over the garlic bulbs and replace the top. Wrap the bulb in aluminum foil and bake for 1 hour. Open the foil, exposing the garlic bulb, and bake for another 1/2 hour. Squeeze cloves out of the garlic bulb and set aside.

In a large saucepan, heat 2 teaspoons of ~~olive oil~~ broth. Add the onion, carrot, and celery and sauté until tender. Add the roasted garlic, potato, and vegetable stock. Bring to a boil, reduce heat, cover, and simmer for 45 minutes.

Chill in refrigerator until cool.

Once cooled, add chopped sorrel and purée. Season with salt and pepper. Serve cold.

Per serving: 111 calories; 3 g protein; 18 g carbohydrate; 3.5 g fat; 2 g fiber; 40 mg calcium; 530 mg sodium; calories from protein: 9%; calories from carbohydrates: 65%; calories from fats: 26%

BUTTERNUT SOUP WITH CINNAMON CREAM

The Lanesborough, London, England

SERVES 4

*T*he Lanesborough serves up nouvelle cuisine in a pretty, airy setting surprisingly found inside a staid, imposing hotel with a prestigious London address. The soymilk helps lighten the ingredient list for this delectable "cream" soup.

2 tablespoons ~~olive oil~~ *broth*
1 onion, finely chopped
2 pounds butternut squash, peeled and chopped
1 carrot, chopped
4 centimeter (1-1/2 inch) piece fresh root ginger, grated

1/2 teaspoon ground cinnamon
1 tablespoon ground coriander
3 cups vegetable stock
1 cup soymilk
salt and freshly ground pepper to taste

In a heavy-bottomed pan, heat the ~~olive oil~~ *broth* and sauté the onion over medium heat for 5 minutes until golden. Add the squash, carrot, ginger, cinnamon, and coriander. Sauté over a medium heat, stirring for 5-8 minutes until the vegetables are browned.

Add the vegetable stock and soymilk and bring to a boil. Reduce the heat to medium and cook, stirring for 30-35 minutes until the vegetables are tender. Blend until smooth in a blender or food processor. Season with salt and pepper.

Per serving: 218 calories; 6 g protein; 35 g carbohydrate; 9 g fat; 5 g fiber; 122 mg calcium; 773 mg sodium; calories from protein: 7%; calories from carbohydrates: 60%; calories from fats: 33%

CURRIED SPROUTING BEAN SOUP

The George, Brighton, England

MAKES ABOUT 2 QUARTS

*T*he George is simply *The George*. A classic, noisy English pub whose "bangers and mash" (sausage and mashed potatoes) are vegan and eaten with relish (and a tankard of Grolsch) by the eclectic clientele. It also serves up a tremendous sprouted bean soup.

1 tablespoon vegetable oil *broth*
2 medium onions, chopped
2 stalks celery, chopped
2 large cloves garlic, crushed
2 teaspoons ginger, finely chopped
1 chili pepper, finely sliced
1/4 teaspoon each: turmeric, ground coriander, cinnamon, cardamom seeds (pods discarded)

1 teaspoon cumin
1 bay leaf
1-1/2 cups sprouted* dried beans, or 2 cups cooked beans
6 cups vegetable stock**
salt and pepper to taste
chopped fresh cilantro (garnish)

Heat the ~~oil~~ *broth* in a large saucepan. Add the onions and cook to soften over medium heat. Add the celery and cook for another 4-5 minutes until the onions start to brown. Add the garlic, ginger, and chili pepper and cook until these start to soften. If vegetables start to stick, add a small amount of the vegetable stock.

Add the remaining spices and the bay leaf. Stir constantly until you can smell all the aromatic flavors rising from the pan. Then add the beans to the onion and spice mix, coating them well.

Pour the vegetable stock over the beans, cover the pan, and bring to a boil. Reduce heat and simmer for 45 minutes, or until the beans are tender. The cooking time will vary according to the type of beans you use.

Ladle out 2 cups of strained beans and vegetables from the soup and purée in a food processor, then return the purée to the soup. This will give the soup its thickness while keeping many of the beans whole for an interesting texture.

Season and serve with a garnish of fresh coriander.

SPROUTING THE BEANS

Almost all dry beans can be sprouted. The best-known sprouting beans are the mung beans used extensively in Chinese cooking. Adzukis, lentils, chickpeas, and soybeans are also commonly used.

Wash the beans with lukewarm water. Place them in a large bowl and cover with warm water that measures about 3 times their depth. Place the bowl in a warm, dark place, such as on top of the refrigerator, covered with a towel. Soak for 12 to 24 hours. Drain the beans and place them into four separate 1-liter pickling jars with equal portions per jar. Cover the jars with cheesecloth or a fine mesh screen, and secure with elastic or string. Lay the jar sideways and spread the beans evenly against the sides of the jar wall. This will expose the bean surface area to better air circulation. Keep them warm and moist in the dark (cover with a dish towel if needed). Rinse the beans 3-4 times per day to prevent them from becoming musty or moldy. Drain thoroughly each time you rinse. After 4 days, uncover the sprouts, allowing them indirect light. Continue to rinse and drain as the tail grows. The sprout should be between 2 to 3 inches in length. Once sprouted, keep refrigerated.

* If time doesn't permit sprouting beans and 2 cups of cooked beans are used instead, the cooking time after adding the beans is reduced to 30 minutes.

** For a lower sodium soup, replace some or all of the vegetable stock with water.

Per serving using cooked beans: 144 calories; 8.5 g protein; 22.8 g carbohydrate; 3.6 g fat; 5 g fiber; 70 mg calcium; 1017 mg sodium; calories from protein: 21%; calories from carbohydrates: 60%; calories from fats: 19%

Salads

ASPARAGUS & TEMPEH SALAD
WITH CHILI SESAME DRESSING

Manna Vegetarian Restaurant, London, England

SERVES 4

This is the oldest vegetarian dinner restaurant in England and resembles a Swiss chalet. Just up a side street from Regent's Park Road, Manna serves countless delights like this asparagus salad.

DRESSING

zest and juice of 1 lime
juice of 1 lemon
3 tablespoons olive oil*
1 tablespoon toasted sesame oil
1 red chili, deseeded and finely sliced
1/2 teaspoon paprika

1 clove garlic, finely chopped
4 teaspoons maple syrup
1 teaspoon soy sauce
1 tablespoon finely chopped coriander leaf (cilantro)
Tabasco to taste

TEMPEH

8 ounces tempeh
3 tablespoons soy sauce
3 tablespoons water

1 clove garlic, sliced
2 teaspoons vegetable oil
1 tablespoon toasted sesame oil

ASPARAGUS

1 teaspoon sesame oil
1 red pepper, cut into strips
2 spring onions, finely sliced diagonally

1 clove garlic, minced
1 pound asparagus, trimmed and cut in half

4 cups chopped butter lettuce

coriander leaf (cilantro)

For the dressing: Mix all ingredients together, stir well, and leave for at least 30 minutes for the flavors to develop.

For the tempeh: Cut tempeh into triangles, 2-inches long and 1/2-inch thick. Mix the soy sauce with water and the sliced garlic. Briefly dip the tempeh into the marinade and then fry in the mixed vegetable and sesame oils until golden brown.

For the asparagus: Heat the sesame oil over medium-high heat. Add the peppers, onion, and garlic. Stir-fry until tender. Add the asparagus and cook until dark green and slightly tender.

Place lettuce on plates. Put the asparagus mixture and tempeh on top in an appealing way. Shake the dressing until well-mixed and dress the salad. Garnish with a little extra coriander.

* *For a lower fat dressing, use 3 tablespoons of rice vinegar instead of olive oil.*

Per serving: 520 calories; 16.3 g protein; 26 g carbohydrate; 41.5 g fat; 3 g fiber; 110 mg calcium; 883 mg sodium; calories from protein: 11%; calories from carbohydrates: 19%; calories from fats: 70%

MOROCCAN EGGPLANT SALAD

Millennium, San Francisco, California

SERVES 6

SALAD

2 Italian eggplants, cut into 1/3-inch matchsticks
2 tomatoes, cut into 1/3-inch cubes
1 cup cooked chickpeas or any firm-textured bean
1 bunch scallions, white part only, chopped
1/2 cup chopped, preserved lemons (recipe follows)
1-1/2 cups Moroccan Dressing (recipe follows)
1 bunch cilantro, stemmed and chopped
1/3 bunch mint, stemmed and chopped
leaves from 1 head romaine lettuce, shredded

Soak the eggplant in warm, salted water for 15 minutes. Drain and then blanch in boiling water until tender, about 5 minutes. Drain and transfer to an ice water bath. When cool, drain well. In a medium bowl, combine the eggplant with all the remaining ingredients except for the shredded romaine. Serve over the shredded romaine lettuce.

PRESERVED LEMONS

MAKES 24 WEDGES

4 lemons, each cut into 6 wedges   1 tablespoon sea salt
1/2 cup fresh lemon juice

Place the lemon wedges in a clean, 1-quart heavy glass or ceramic container with a large opening. Add the lemon juice and salt and mix well with the lemons. Add warm water to cover the lemons. Cover the surface of the mixture with plastic wrap and top with a saucer to weigh down the lemons and keep them submerged. Let sit at room temperature for 5 days. After 5 days the lemons will be ready for use, though 3-4 more days will make softer, less pungent lemons. To store, refrigerate the preserved lemons in their brine for up to 2 weeks. To use, rinse the lemon wedges of excess brine and salt.

MOROCCAN DRESSING

MAKES 2-1/2 CUPS

2 teaspoons ground cumin
1 teaspoon ground coriander
2 teaspoons Spanish paprika
1/2 cup fresh lemon juice (about 4 lemons)
1 tablespoon balsamic vinegar
2 teaspoons minced fresh ginger
2 teaspoons minced garlic

1/3 cup chopped fresh cilantro
1/2 cup light olive oil (or 4 ounces low-fat silken tofu and 1 tablespoon light miso)
1/3 cup water (1/2 cup if replacing olive oil with tofu and miso)
2 teaspoons sea salt
1 teaspoon ground pepper

In a dry, small sauté pan or skillet, toast the cumin, coriander, and paprika over medium heat until the spices become fragrant and the color slightly darkens, about 1 minute. In a blender, combine the toasted spices with the lemon juice, vinegar, ginger, garlic, and cilantro. With the machine running, gradually add the oil and then the water, salt, and pepper. Leftover dressing will keep in the refrigerator for up to a week.

Per serving (with oil dressing): 274 calories; 7 g protein; 30 g carbohydrate; 14 g fat; 9 g fiber; 26 mg calcium; 585 mg sodium; calories from protein: 10%; calories from carbohydrates: 44%; calories from fats: 46%

Per serving (with oil-free dressing): 196 calories; 7 g protein; 32 g carbohydrate; 4 g fat; 9 g fiber; 32 mg calcium; 665 mg sodium; calories from protein: 15%; calories from carbohydrates: 66%; calories from fats: 19%

GUNDEL SALAD

Gundel, Budapest, Hungary

SERVES 4

The Gundel chef has carefully altered the famous Gundel Salad, created more than 50 years ago, adjusting it to modern tastes.

1 pound mushrooms, wiped clean with a paper towel, trimmed, and quartered
salt and black pepper to taste
juice of 1 lemon
2 tablespoons balsamic vinegar
2 tablespoons rice or white wine vinegar
1 teaspoon granulated sugar
1-2 tablespoons olive oil
1 tablespoon vegan Worcestershire sauce
2 tablespoons chopped fresh parsley
4 red or yellow bell peppers

1 pound asparagus (preferably white asparagus)
8 cups water
1 tablespoon granulated sugar
pinch of salt
pinch of baking soda
8 ounces green or yellow beans, trimmed and cut into 1-inch lengths
4 tomatoes
1 cucumber
2 heads Boston lettuce
12 dandelion leaves or other bitter greens such as arugula or watercress

Preheat oven to 450°F.

Put the mushrooms in a bowl. Add salt and black pepper to taste, lemon juice, vinegars, sugar, olive oil, Worcestershire sauce, and parsley. Mix carefully to avoid mashing the mushrooms. Cover and refrigerate for at least 30 minutes. At the same time, put 4 salad plates in the refrigerator.

Put bell peppers in a baking pan and bake in the oven. After 4 minutes, transfer the peppers to a small paper bag, seal, and set aside for 10 minutes. Then peel the peppers, remove seeds, and slice. Put the peppers on a plate and sprinkle with 3 tablespoons of the liquid accumulated in the bowl holding the mushrooms.

Trim 1/2-inch from the bottom of the asparagus stems, if necessary. (If the asparagus are not young and tender, peel the stems.) Snap or cut the asparagus into 1-inch lengths. In a large pot, bring 4 cups of water to a boil. Add the sugar and lower the heat. Then add the asparagus and simmer until tender. Cool the asparagus in its cooking water for 5 minutes and then remove from the water and set on a plate to cool further. After 15 minutes, put the asparagus in the refrigerator for at least 30 minutes to chill.

In another pot, bring 4 cups of water to a boil. Add a pinch of salt and baking soda. Cook the green beans in the water for 3 minutes. Cool the green beans in the

cooking water for 2 minutes and then remove from water and set on a plate to cool further. After 15 minutes, put beans in the refrigerator for at least 30 minutes to chill.

Put the tomatoes in another pot of boiling water for about 1 minute until the skins crack. Remove from the boiling water and plunge into a bowl of cold water. Peel the tomatoes and cube them.

Halve the cucumber lengthwise, remove seeds with a spoon, and slice into 1/4-inch pieces. Put the sliced cucumber in a bowl and add a pinch of salt with 3 tablespoons of the liquid accumulated in the bowl holding the mushrooms.

Core and clean the lettuce and greens. Tear into bite-sized pieces. Wash and drain.

To serve, put a pile of the torn lettuce and greens on the chilled plates and drizzle with 2 tablespoons of the liquid accumulated in the bowl holding the mushrooms. Arrange the cooled vegetables, including the mushrooms, on the lettuce, alternating the colors. Drizzle with the remaining mushroom liquid, dividing equally among the plates.

Per serving: 288 calories; 12 g protein; 45 g carbohydrate; 8 g fat; 13 g fiber; 159 mg calcium; 120 mg sodium; calories from protein: 16%; calories from carbohydrates: 61%; calories from fats: 23%

BUTTERNUT SQUASH, ROASTED CORN AND TOMATILLO SALAD

Second Helpings, New York, New York

SERVES 8

*T*omatillos are small, firm, tomato-like fruits that come in a variety of colors ranging from bright green to purple and are enclosed in brown husks. They have a tart, lemony flavor that develops during cooking and are common in many Mexican and Southwestern sauces and salsas.

SALAD

1 cup roasted corn*
1 cup peeled, diced, and boiled butternut squash

1 cup cooked black-eyed peas
1 cup roasted tomatillos*

DRESSING

1 cup roasted tomatillos*
2 cloves garlic
1 small bunch cilantro, about 3/4 cup
sea salt and pepper to taste

2 tablespoons extra virgin olive oil
warm water (optional)
juice of 1 lime (optional)

Combine salad ingredients in a bowl.

For the dressing: Blend tomatillos, garlic, cilantro, salt, and pepper in a food processor or blender until smooth. Add olive oil and blend to create a thick dressing. A little warm water may be added if the dressing is too thick. Lime juice may also be added to create an extra tangy flavor.

Toss salad with dressing. Serve at room temperature.

* *To roast corn, place the kernels in a dry, cast-iron pan over medium flame and roast until lightly blackened. To roast tomatillos, remove the husks, place them in a broiler, and broil until lightly blackened.*

Per serving: 87 calories; 3 g protein; 13 g carbohydrate; 4 g fat; 2.5 g fiber; 20 mg calcium; 182 mg sodium; calories from protein: 9%; calories from carbohydrates: 54%; calories from fats: 37%

MILLENNIUM CAESAR SALAD

Millennium, San Francisco, California

SERVES 6

*T*his is Millennium's version of the classic. The combination of capers and nutritional yeast gives this dressing the pungent bite and body that eludes many Caesar dressings. If nutritional yeast in unavailable, add 1/4 cup bread that has been soaked in water to thicken the dressing.

SALAD

3 heads romaine lettuce (all but the very outermost leaves)
1-1/2 cups Oil-Free Croutons (recipe follows)

1-1/2 cups Caesar Dressing (recipe follows) or Oil-Free Caesar Dressing (recipe follows)
1 carrot, peeled and shredded

Tear the lettuce leaves into bite-sized pieces. In a large bowl, toss the lettuce and croutons with the dressing. Divide among 6 salad plates and top with the shredded carrot.

 OIL-FREE CROUTONS

MAKES 4 CUPS

2 cups slightly stale bread cubes
1/4 cup water
1/2 teaspoon each: dried oregano, dried thyme, dried basil, paprika, sea salt

Preheat the oven to 350°F.

In a medium bowl, combine all the ingredients and toss well. Spread the breadcrumbs on a baking sheet and bake, turning every 5 minutes, for 15 minutes, or until the bread cubes are crisp and dry. Let cool to room temperature. Store in an airtight container for up to 1 week.

CAESAR DRESSING

MAKES 1-3/4 CUPS

1 cup fresh lemon juice
2 cloves garlic, minced
2 teaspoons drained capers
1 tablespoon Dijon mustard
2 teaspoons nutritional yeast

1/2 teaspoon ground pepper
1/2 cup extra virgin olive oil
1 cup canola oil or light olive oil
sea salt to taste

In a blender, combine the lemon juice, garlic, capers, mustard, yeast, pepper, and extra virgin olive oil. Blend until smooth. With the machine running, gradually add the canola oil in a thick stream until incorporated. Add the sea salt. Store in an airtight container in the refrigerator for up to 1 week.

OIL-FREE CAESAR DRESSING

MAKES 2 CUPS

1 12.3-ounce package low-fat silken tofu
3/4 cup fresh lemon juice
1-2 cloves garlic, minced
3 tablespoons drained capers

1/4 cup nutritional yeast
2 tablespoons Dijon mustard
1/4 teaspoon ground pepper
1 cup water
sea salt to taste

In a blender, purée all of the ingredients until smooth. Taste and adjust the seasonings. Thin with more water if needed to reach the desired consistency. Store in an airtight container in the refrigerator for up to 1 week.

Per serving (with oil dressing): 512 calories; 4 g protein; 16 g carbohydrate; 48 g fat; 3 g fiber; 30 mg calcium; 270 mg sodium; calories from protein: 3%; calories from carbohydrates: 13%; calories from fats: 84%

Per serving (with oil-free dressing): 114 calories; 7 g protein; 17 g carbohydrate; 2 g fat; 3 g fiber; 47 mg calcium; 531 mg sodium; calories from protein: 24%; calories from carbohydrates: 60%; calories from fats: 16%

CHILLED SOBA NOODLE SALAD

Millennium, San Francisco, California

SERVES 6

Among America's leading restaurants, Millennium has one of the most thoughtful and creative menus anywhere. This salad is a popular summer dish. The addition of fresh peach and arame make it unique.

DRESSING

1 cup fresh lemon juice
1/3 cup tamari or soy sauce
1 tablespoon Sucanat®
1 tablespoon ketchup

1/4 teaspoon red pepper flakes
1 teaspoon minced, fermented black beans (optional)
2 kaffir lime leaves, minced or finely

1/2 cup water or vegetable stock
1/4 cup toasted sesame seeds
3 tablespoons minced fresh ginger
  shredded (optional)

2 tablespoons Asian sesame oil
  (optional)

SALAD

6 ounces soba noodles
kernels cut from 2 ears of sweet corn
1 peach, peeled, pitted, and thinly sliced
4-6 snow peas, julienned
4 ounces packaged smoked tofu
2 tablespoons soaked and drained arame sea vegetables
1-1/2 cups shredded romaine lettuce, or 6 ounces mixed baby greens
3 tablespoons julienned scallions, white part only
3 tablespoons julienned Thai or Italian basil leaves
12-18 cherry tomatoes

For the dressing: In a small bowl, whisk all the dressing ingredients together. Store in an airtight container in the refrigerator for up to 2 weeks.

For the salad: Cook the noodles in boiling, salted water for 6-8 minutes, until al denté. Drain and set aside to cool.

Toss the noodles, corn, peach, snow peas, tofu, and arame sea vegetables with the dressing. Divide the shredded romaine or mixed greens among 6 salad plates. Top with a mound of the noodle mixture. Top the salads with scallion and basil, arranging the tomatoes around the plates.

Per serving (with oil): 208 calories; 7 g protein; 27 g carbohydrate; 8 g fat; 3 g fiber; 142 mg calcium; 781 mg sodium; calories from protein: 13%; calories from carbohydrates: 52%; calories from fats: 35%

Per serving (without oil): 172 calories; 7 g protein; 27 g carbohydrate; 4 g fat; 3 g fiber; 142 mg calcium; 781 mg sodium; calories from protein: 16%; calories from carbohydrates: 63%; calories from fats: 21%

Main Dishes

TAGLIATELLE AUX GIROLLES

Au Fil à la Pâte, Ramatuelle, France

SERVES 4

*F*amilies and yachting visitors can escape for delicious mushroom pasta and local wine at this small, warm, friendly restaurant near St. Tropez. Girolles are mushrooms popular in the south of France. If girolles are not available, shiitake mushrooms can be used instead.

2 tablespoons pine nuts	salt and pepper to taste
30 fresh basil leaves, or approximately 1 cup packed leaves	1 cup olive oil*
2 tablespoons vegan parmesan cheese or nutritional yeast	1 pound Tagliatelle noodles
7 cloves garlic	non-stick cooking spray
	2 cups sliced girolles (also called "chanterelles")

Whoa, Too Much! (handwritten annotation)

Preheat oven to 375°F.

Place the pine nuts on a baking sheet and bake for about 3 minutes, or until lightly browned. Remove from oven and set aside.

In a food processor, add the basil, vegan parmesan cheese, garlic, salt, and pepper. Start to blend and slowly drizzle in the oil until the mixture is blended.

Cook the pasta according to package directions. Drain the pasta, reserving about 1-2 tablespoons of the cooking liquid.

Heat a small skillet over medium heat. Spray with non-stick cooking spray. Add the girolles and sauté for 3-4 minutes. Remove from heat.

Place the cooked pasta in a large serving bowl. Add the basil mixture and toss gently. Top with girolles. Serve immediately.

* For a lower fat version, replace some of the olive oil with water.

Per serving: 944 calories; 17 g protein; 90 g carbohydrate; 59 g fat; 6 g fiber; 93 mg calcium; 67 mg sodium; calories from protein: 7%; calories from carbohydrates: 38%; calories from fats: 55%

ASPARAGUS RISOTTO

TJ's Restaurant & Lounge, Richmond, Virginia

SERVES 4

A lively and popular social destination in the very grand Jefferson Hotel, TJ's Restaurant & Lounge offers imaginative food in an informal atmosphere.

Using a mixture of yellow and red tomatoes in this dish gives it a festive look.

6 cups vegetable broth
2 tablespoons oil
1 small onion, diced
2-4 cloves garlic, thinly sliced
1-1/2 cups uncooked arborio rice
1/2 cup dry white wine
1 pound asparagus, trimmed and bias
    cut into 1-inch pieces

zest and juice of 1 lemon
1/4 cup extra virgin olive oil*
1 tablespoon shredded fresh basil
1 tablespoon chopped fresh tarragon
1/2 cup diced fresh tomato
salt and white pepper to taste

Heat the vegetable broth over low heat on a burner near the risotto pan. Have a ladle handy.

Heat the oil in a large, wide skillet over medium-high heat and sauté the onion, garlic, and rice. Cook, stirring constantly, until the rice begins to brown. Do not let more than one-tenth of the rice brown. Add the wine and cook, stirring, until the rice absorbs the liquid. Add 1 cup of the stock. Reduce the heat to medium. Cook, stirring, until most of the stock is absorbed. Do not allow the rice to brown or stick to the pan. Continue adding the stock, 1 cup at a time, and cook until it is nearly all absorbed. When adding the last cup of stock, add the asparagus.

When the stock is absorbed and the asparagus is just tender, remove the pan from the heat. Stir in the lemon juice, half the zest, 3 tablespoons of olive oil, the herbs, and tomatoes. Mix gently so the asparagus doesn't fall apart. Taste for seasoning and add salt and white pepper as needed.

Divide the risotto among four large, shallow bowls. Garnish with the reserved basil and top with some lemon zest. Drizzle a teaspoon or so of the extra virgin olive oil. Serve immediately.

For a lower fat version, skip drizzling the final dish with additional olive oil.

Per serving: 352 calories; 8 g protein; 31 g carbohydrate; 22 g fat; 3.4 g fiber; 43 mg calcium; 1508 mg sodium; calories from protein: 8%; calories from carbohydrates: 34%; calories from fats: 54%; calories from alcohol: 4%

SEAWEED TOFU BURGER

The Great 844 Store Café, Kyoto City, Japan

MAKES 8-12 BURGERS

25 ounces extra-firm tofu
1 ounce dried hijiki seaweed
2 medium potatoes
4 green onions
1 medium carrot
3 shiitake mushroom tops
1 tablespoon sesame oil
2 teaspoons soy sauce

2 tablespoons miso
pinch of salt and pepper
1-1/2 cups breadcrumbs
bread
lettuce (sandwich topping)
alfalfa sprouts (sandwich topping)
teriyaki or soy sauce (sandwich topping)

Preheat oven to 375°F.

Place the tofu on a plate. Put another plate on top and place in the refrigerator for 1-3 hours to drain the water out of the tofu.

Soak the hijiki in water for 20 minutes.

Boil the potatoes for about as long as you would when making a potato salad.

Finely chop the green onions, carrot, and shiitake mushrooms, then lightly fry in the sesame oil. Add the soy sauce.

Put the tofu in a food processor and blend with miso, salt, and pepper. Next, add the potato and blend slightly, so the potato mixes but doesn't lose its form.

Place the tofu mixture in a bowl and stir in the hijiki, onions, carrots, and mushrooms. Divide into either 8 or 12 balls. Mix each with about 2 tablespoons of breadcrumbs, mold into burger shapes, and lightly fry on both sides.

Place the burgers on a baking sheet and bake for 10 minutes.

Warm the bread and chop the lettuce.

Make sandwiches with the burgers and vegetables, sprinkling teriyaki or soy sauce on top.

Per serving: 281 calories; 13 g protein; 37 g carbohydrate; 8 g fat; 4.5 g fiber; 145 mg calcium; 1036 mg sodium; calories from protein: 19%; calories from carbohydrates: 55%; calories from fats: 26%

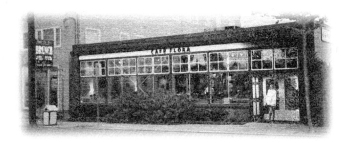

CAFÉ FLORA WILD MUSHROOM CURRY WITH THAI RED CURRY PASTE

Café Flora, Seattle, Washington

SERVES 4

*T*he floorshow at Café Flora is watching the enormous salads of fresh garden ingredients being prepared at the counter. You'll fall in love with the light, airy rooms with huge open windows where you can enjoy a satisfying variety of healthy, tasty fare beautifully presented.

The inspiration for Café Flora's Wild Mushroom Curry was a sudden abundance of lobster mushrooms from one of their foragers. Lobster mushrooms have a unique ocean scent and flavor when cooked. Unfortunately, these mushrooms are available sporadically, but any other "meaty" mushroom will do, such as shiitake. This curry can incorporate anything you want, such as cooked baby potatoes or tofu. It is great ladled in deep bowls over a heap of thin rice noodles or Jasmine rice.

1 14-ounce can coconut milk*
1 teaspoon Café Flora Thai Red Curry Paste (see directions below; 1 teaspoon for mild, 1-1/2 teaspoons for medium, 2 teaspoons for hot)
3 tablespoons tamari or soy sauce
1/8 teaspoon turmeric
2 teaspoons tamarind concentrate
1 tablespoon vegetable oil
2 medium yellow onions, peeled and thinly sliced
4 large carrots, peeled and thinly cut at an angle

2 pounds mushrooms (shiitake, crimini, chanterelle, lobster, portabella; note: remove stems from shiitake or portabella)
2 large red bell peppers, deseeded and cut in strips
8 ounces cooked rice noodles or jasmine rice, to serve
lime wedges, cilantro, and Thai basil (garnish)

Whisk together the coconut milk with the Thai Red Curry Paste, tamari, turmeric, and tamarind.

Heat the oil in a wok or large, non-stick skillet until very hot. Add the onions and toss lightly over high heat for 2 minutes. Add the carrots and stir constantly for another minute. Add the mushrooms and peppers and cook, stirring constantly, for another minute. If the vegetables start to stick, add a small amount of water or vegetable broth. Add the coconut milk mixture to the vegetables and bring to a boil. Lower heat, stir gently, and allow to simmer for a few more minutes.

Serve over rice or noodles. Garnish with lime wedges, cilantro, and Thai basil.

CAFÉ FLORA THAI RED CURRY PASTE

MAKES 1 CUP

2 tablespoons coriander seed
1 tablespoon toasted cumin seed
1/2 cup crushed red pepper flakes
1 tablespoon hijiki seaweed
2 tablespoons hot water
2 tablespoons fresh ginger
1/4 cup garlic
1/4 cup shallots
2 tablespoons lime juice, or 3 lime leaves (usually available in frozen form at Asian markets)
1 stalk lemongrass

Grind the coriander, cumin, and red pepper flakes in batches using a spice grinder. Then grind the hijiki. Cover the hijiki with hot water and set aside. Peel and chop the ginger, garlic, and shallots. If you are using lime leaves, chop them as well. Cut the bottom stems off the lemongrass and slice very thinly at an angle from the bottom up the stalk until you get to the green part where the stem gets hollow. Chop the lemongrass slices as finely as possible. Put all the ingredients in a food processor and process by first pulsing until you have the mixture going and then turning on the process fully, drizzling in some oil to keep the mixture moving. Process until you have a smooth paste.

Store in the refrigerator or freezer.

* For a lower fat version, replace half of the coconut milk with plain soymilk.

Per serving: 477 calories; 14 g protein; 47 g carbohydrate; 32 g fat; 8 g fiber; 62 mg calcium; 826 mg sodium; calories from protein: 8%; calories from carbohydrates: 36%; calories from fats: 56%

FIVE-FLAVORED TOFU

TJ's Restaurant & Lounge, Richmond, Virginia

SERVES 4

This flavorful tofu is delicious when paired with aromatic jasmine rice.

1/4 cup ketchup
2 tablespoons soy sauce
2 teaspoons lemon juice
1 teaspoon sesame oil
1 pound extra-firm tofu, cut into
1/2-inch cubes
1 tablespoon vegetable oil
4 scallions, trimmed and bias cut into
1-inch pieces
1 teaspoon minced fresh garlic
1 teaspoon grated fresh ginger
1/4 teaspoon crushed red pepper
flakes, or 1 small dried chili
1 green bell pepper, trimmed and cut
into long, thin strips

1 red bell pepper, trimmed and cut
into long, thin strips
1 yellow bell pepper, trimmed and
cut into long, thin strips
4 ounces of shiitake mushrooms,
destemmed and cut into long strips
1 tablespoon chopped fresh basil,
preferably Thai basil, or 1 teaspoon
dried basil
1 tablespoon chopped fresh cilantro
white and/or black sesame seeds
(garnish)

Mix the ketchup with the soy sauce, lemon juice, and sesame oil. Reserve.

Bring a small pot of water to a simmer. Gently add the tofu to the pot and simmer while you are cooking the rest of the dish.

Heat the oil over high heat in a wok or wide saucepan until it just begins to smoke. Add the scallions, garlic, ginger, chilies, peppers, and mushroom and stir-fry until the peppers have just softened. Add the sauce and toss until the mixture is well coated. Add the tofu and herbs and mix gently.

Garnish with white and/or black sesame seeds.

Per serving: 228 calories; 14 g protein; 18 g carbohydrate; 11 g fat; 3 g fiber; 88 mg calcium; 730 mg sodium; calories from protein: 24%; calories from carbohydrates: 32%; calories from fats: 44%

GNOCCHI AUX CÊPES

Le Rive Droit, Nice, France

SERVES 4

*U*sing vegetable broth and miso enhances flavors while diminishing the fat content of the mushroom sauce.

GNOCCHI

1 pound russet potatoes
3/4 cup flour

1/4 teaspoon salt

MUSHROOM SAUCE

2 teaspoons peanut oil
1 garlic clove, minced
8 ounces gourmet mushroom blend
   (shiitake, portabella, etc.), chopped

1 cup vegetable broth
1 cup water
1 teaspoon miso
1 tablespoon cornstarch

For the gnocchi: Preheat oven to 400°F. Bake the potatoes in oven for 50 minutes, or until tender. Peel the potatoes, then place in a food processor. Blend until smooth. Add flour and salt, then process. Turn the dough onto a lightly floured surface. Knead, adding flour if too sticky. Roll the dough into 1/2-inch-thick ropes. Cut the ropes into 1/2-inch pieces. Fold the pieces in half and press a fork into the edges to form ridges. Bring a large pot of lightly salted water to boil. Add the gnocchi, a few at a time. Cook until the gnocchi floats. Remove and drain.

For the mushroom sauce: Heat 2 teaspoons of oil in saucepan over medium-high heat. Add the garlic and mushrooms. Cook until tender. Add the vegetable broth. Reduce heat and simmer. Meanwhile, combine the water, miso, and cornstarch in a small bowl. Add the miso mixture to the saucepan, stirring until thickened.

Place a few gnocchi on a plate and top with mushroom sauce.

Per serving: 222 calories; 7 g protein; 42 g carbohydrate; 3 g fat; 4 g fiber; 31 mg calcium; 456 mg sodium; calories from protein: 12%; calories from carbohydrates: 76%; calories from fats: 12%

SPINACH & "CREAM CHEESE" DUMPLINGS SERVED ON A BED OF PASTA WITH PICKLED TOMATO SAUCE

The 13ᵗʰ Note Café, Glasgow, Scotland

SERVES 4

*A*chic club and restaurant that serves out-of-this-world vegan fare.

DUMPLINGS

1 small red onion
1 tub (8 ounces) Tofutti® plain cream cheese or other brand soy cream cheese*
2 cloves garlic, crushed

1-1/2 cups breadcrumbs
10 ounces spinach, washed and steamed
1/4 teaspoon freshly grated nutmeg
salt and pepper to taste

PICKLED TOMATO SAUCE

2-1/2 red onions, finely diced
2 cloves garlic, crushed
2 tablespoons olive oil
1 tablespoon tomato paste
3 pounds tomatoes, chopped and skinned, or 1 28-ounce can crushed tomatoes with 21 ounces water

3 tablespoons fresh basil
2 tablespoons fresh oregano
2 teaspoons raspberry vinegar
salt and pepper to taste

1 pound pasta of choice

For the dumplings: Finely dice the onion and mix with the other ingredients. Place the mixture in the refrigerator for 30 minutes. Just before cooking, form into golf-ball-sized dumplings and roll in flour. Shallow-fry the dumplings in olive oil, turning occasionally until brown and cooked through.

For the tomato sauce: Sauté the onion and garlic in olive oil, then add the tomato paste once the onions turn transparent. Add the chopped, skinned tomatoes (or crushed tomatoes plus water), basil, and oregano, and simmer for 20 minutes. Add the vinegar and allow to cook for five minutes. Season to taste.

Serve the dumplings on a bed of fresh pasta and spoon over the sauce. Garnish with fresh basil.

For a lower fat version, replace half the Tofutti® cream cheese with 4 ounces of extra-firm tofu. Combine the soy cream cheese and tofu in a food processor until smooth.

Per serving: 732 calories; 22 g protein; 106 g carbohydrate; 27 g fat; 16 g fiber; 155 mg calcium; 1091 mg sodium; calories from protein: 12%; calories from carbohydrates: 57%; calories from fats: 31%

RAVIOLI AUF TOMATENSUGO

Griechenbeisl, Vienna, Austria

SERVES 10

*T*omato sauce can be made a day in advance to help break up the preparation time, while letting the sauce flavors marry. Just keep it refrigerated and then heat in a saucepan when needed. Replacing the eggs with Egg Replacer® and the parmesan cheese with either nutritional yeast or vegan parmesan cheese makes this a heart-healthy Austrian experience.

TOMATO SAUCE

2 15-ounce cans diced tomatoes
2 medium yellow onions, chopped
3 cloves garlic
2 tablespoons olive oil

1/2 cup chopped fresh basil
pinch of salt and pepper
2 teaspoons sugar

Pour the canned tomatoes into a colander, saving the drained juice. Fry the chopped onions and garlic lightly in olive oil, until tender. Add the tomatoes and juice, and bring to a boil. Add the chopped basil and the salt, pepper, and sugar to taste. Set aside and let flavors marry while preparing the filling and raviolis.

RAVIOLI

2-1/4 cups hard wheat or semolina
   flour
1/3 cup water

Egg Replacer®, equivalent to 2 eggs
2 tablespoons olive oil
1 teaspoon salt

In a large bowl, use a wooden spoon to stir the flour with the remaining ingredients to make a stiff dough. On a well-floured surface, knead the dough until it is smooth and not sticky. Wrap the dough with plastic wrap and let it sit for 30 minutes for easier rolling.

FILLING

1/2 cup finely chopped celery
3/4 cup finely chopped carrots
3/4 cup finely chopped turnips
3/4 cup finely chopped leeks
1 tablespoon chopped parsley

1 tablespoon olive oil
pinch of salt
1/4 cup silken tofu
1/4 cup nutritional yeast or vegan
   parmesan cheese

Make the ravioli filling by lightly frying the celery, carrots, turnips, leeks, and parsley in a pan with olive oil. Add the salt and mix with the tofu and nutritional yeast or vegan parmesan cheese.

Separate the dough into 4 pieces. On a floured surface and with floured rolling pin, roll one piece into a rectangle. Keep the remaining dough covered. With the dull edge of a knife, lightly mark the dough into 2-inch squares; place a scant teaspoon of filling in the center of each. Roll the second piece of dough into the same sized rectangle and place it over the filling. Press around the filling and along the edges. With a pastry wheel or knife, cut into the ravioli; place on a floured, clean cloth towel. Repeat with the remaining dough and filling. Let the ravioli dry for 30 minutes before boiling.

TO SERVE

1/4 cup nutritional yeast or vegan parmesan cheese to sprinkle over ravioli and
   sauce

Bring about 6 quarts of water to a boil. Add ravioli. Stir gently to separate the pieces. Remove them with a slotted spoon when they rise to the top. Serve them directly with the tomato sauce and sprinkled with nutritional yeast or vegan parmesan cheese.

Per serving: 212 calories; 5 g protein; 32 g carbohydrate; 8 g fat; 3 g fiber; 63 mg calcium; 260 mg sodium; calories from protein: 9%; calories from carbohydrates: 59%; calories from fats: 32%

STEAMED SEASONED TOFU

Health Haven, Toronto, Canada

SERVES 4

6 dried shiitake mushrooms
1/3 cup coarsely broken vermicelli
   noodles
1 pound soft tofu
3 tablespoons shredded carrot
1/2 teaspoon salt (or to taste)
1 teaspoon sesame oil

1/4 teaspoon pepper
1 teaspoon potato starch
2 tablespoons soy sauce (garnish)
3 tablespoons chopped sea vegetables (nori, hijiki, or arame)
   (garnish)

Soak the mushrooms in warm water for 20-25 minutes, or until soft. Squeeze out excess water. Cut off and discard stems. Slice mushrooms into thin strips.

Soak the vermicelli noodles in hot water for 10 minutes until soft. Drain very well.

Gently mash tofu. Stir in mushrooms, carrot, and vermicelli. Combine and stir in the salt, sesame oil, pepper, and potato starch. Pat the mixture into a lightly greased metal or ceramic bowl just large enough to hold it. Smooth the top. Place the bowl in a large pot filled with 1 inch of water. Cover and bring to a boil. Steam for 12-15 minutes until the tofu firms up slightly.

To serve, turn the bowl upside down onto a plate. Drizzle with soy sauce and then sprinkle with the chopped sea vegetables.

* Serving Suggestion: Before adding the tofu mixture to a bowl, line the bowl with sliced carrots and mushrooms. This will create a beautiful pattern once the bowl is removed.

Per serving: 167 calories; 11 g protein; 19 g carbohydrate; 5 g fat; 2 g fiber; 165 mg calcium; 818 mg sodium; calories from protein: 27%; calories from carbohydrates: 45%; calories from fats: 28%

Artichoke and Forest Cêpe Ravioli

The Painted Table, Seattle, Washington

SERVES 4

*T*his exceptional mushroom and artichoke ravioli dish has been simplified by using lasagna sheets or pasta shells.

3 tablespoons baked garlic purée (see directions below)
4 fresh, medium artichokes, or 1 12-ounce can of artichoke bottoms packed in water
1 large cêpe or portabella mushroom, finely chopped

2 tablespoons fresh, finely chopped herbs (thyme, oregano, chives)
salt and pepper to taste
4 fresh lasagna sheets, or 10-12 jumbo pasta shells

2 cups vegetable stock
1 bunch lemon thyme
1 tablespoon olive oil
1 lemon

salt and pepper to taste
3 cups braising greens (spinach, kale, chard, etc.)

To prepare baked garlic purée: Preheat the oven to 350°F. Slice through the top 1/4 of a medium head of garlic. Open and drizzle the sliced area with a small amount of olive oil. Close up the garlic head and bake uncovered in a small glass or ceramic dish for 30-40 minutes, until soft. Remove from the oven and allow to cool until it is no longer too hot to touch. Use a blunt-ended table knife to remove garlic cloves from the skin. Put all the cloves in a small dish and mash with a fork.

To prepare fresh artichokes: Trim off outer leaves and top 2 inches of the artichokes. Slowly cook in lemon water that has been salted, until tender. When cool to the touch, remove excess leaves until only bottom remains. If using canned artichokes, simply drain and trim off any tough parts. Purée half of the artichoke bottoms and finely dice the rest.

Combine with garlic purée, mushrooms, and herbs. Stir and season with salt and pepper as needed.

To make ravioli: Lay out a sheet of fresh pasta (4- by 12-inches) and place 2 tablespoons of filling every 2 inches in two rows.

44

Lay another sheet on top and crimp with a ravioli cutter. Drop in salted boiling water for 5-6 minutes and drain. If you prefer to stuff ready-made shells, simply cook 10-12 jumbo pasta shells in boiling water according to package directions, drain, and fill.

To make sauce: Simmer the lemon thyme in vegetable stock for 30 minutes to infuse.

Strain and finish with oil, salt, pepper, and a squeeze of fresh lemon. Toss greens with sauce until wilted and add ravioli. Serve immediately.

Per serving: 320 calories; 19 g protein; 53 g carbohydrate; 4 g fat; 21 g fiber; 214 mg calcium; 1244 mg sodium; calories from protein: 23%; calories from carbohydrates: 66%; calories from fats: 11%

Schwammerlgulasch

Griechenbeisl, Vienna, Austria

SERVES 4

$\mathscr{M}$ushroom goulash at its best.

2 teaspoons olive oil *broth*
1 medium onion, chopped
1 medium green or red bell pepper,
  chopped
4 tablespoons tomato paste
2 garlic cloves, minced
1 teaspoon paprika
1 cup vegetable stock
1 cup thick soymilk or soy creamer

1 teaspoon dried basil
1 tablespoon soy sauce
1/2 teaspoon liquid smoke
2 pounds gourmet mushrooms
  (such as portabellas, baby bellas,
  crimini, shiitake), washed and
  chopped into bite-sized pieces
salt and pepper to taste

Heat I teaspoon of oil *broth* in a non-stick Dutch oven over medium-high heat. Lightly stir-fry the chopped onions until tender. Add the chopped bell pepper, tomato paste, and minced garlic and stir-fry a bit more, adding water or vegetable broth as needed to prevent sticking. Remove from heat and allow to cool. Add paprika and the next five ingredients (vegetable stock through liquid smoke) and let simmer for 20 minutes. Meanwhile, heat the remaining teaspoon of oil in a non-stick skillet over medium-high heat. Add the mushrooms and stir-fry until soft. Add the cooked mushrooms to the cooled sauce, then bring to a boil. Add salt and pepper to taste.

Per serving: 175 calories; 11 g protein; 27 g carbohydrate; 4 g fat; 9 g fiber; 58 mg calcium; 572 mg sodium; calories from protein: 22%; calories from carbohydrates: 59%; calories from fats: 19%

Tagine of Vegetables with Charmoula Couscous Fritters

The Lanesborough, London, England

SERVES 4

$\mathscr{T}$agine is a traditional dish made in North Africa. It refers both to the food and the traditional earthenware dish with a conical lid in which it is served. Charmoula is a mix of fragrant herbs, spices, garlic, and oil, often enjoyed in Morocco.

TAGINE

2 teaspoons olive oil
1 red onion, cut into wedges
2 garlic cloves, crushed
8 fat baby carrots, grated
1 teaspoon ground coriander
2 teaspoons harissa paste (Moroccan chili paste)
1 tablespoon tomato paste
2 sweet potatoes, peeled and cut into chunks
2 baking potatoes, peeled and cut into wedges
2 zucchini, thickly sliced on the diagonal
1 14.5-ounce can chopped tomatoes, drained
2 cups vegetable stock
3 tablespoons chopped fresh cilantro

FRITTERS

1 package olive oil-flavored couscous (such as Near East's Roasted Garlic and Olive Oil Couscous®)
1 small garlic clove
1/2 teaspoon ground cumin
1/2 teaspoon ground coriander
2 tablespoons toasted pine nuts
1/4 cup prepared hummus
1/2 cup fine white breadcrumbs
3 tablespoons olive oil*

fresh cilantro (garnish)

For the tagine: Heat the oil in a large pan. Add the onion, garlic, carrots, and ground coriander and cook for 5 minutes over medium heat until just beginning to brown. Add the harissa paste and tomato paste and cook for another 2 minutes.

Add the sweet potatoes, potatoes, and zucchini and stir together. Cook for 2 minutes before adding the chopped tomatoes, vegetable stock, and fresh cilantro. Bring to a boil, cover, and simmer gently for 25-30 minutes until the vegetables are tender and the sauce has thickened.

For the fritters: Prepare the couscous according to package directions. Place cooked couscous, garlic, cumin, coriander, and pine nuts in a food processor. Pulse until combined.

Mix the hummus and breadcrumbs with the couscous and form into patties. Heat the oil in a non-stick skillet over medium-high heat. Add the couscous patties and cook until lightly browned on each side.

Drain the patties on paper towels and keep them hot while you cook the remainder. Season the tagine to taste and serve with the couscous fritters, garnished with the fresh cilantro.

* For a lower fat version, use non-stick cooking spray instead of olive oil.

Per serving: 547 calories; 15 g protein; 86 g carbohydrate; 18 g fat; 9 g fiber; 85 mg calcium; 809 mg sodium; calories from protein: 10%; calories from carbohydrates: 62%; calories from fats: 28%

VERMICELLI DELIGHT

Hangawi, New York, New York

SERVES 6

*A*n elegant restaurant on Manhattan's east side. Diners remove their shoes and sit on the floor, Korean-style, and are greeted by truly extraordinary vegetarian cuisine with exceptional service. Hangawi is among the very best restaurants in New York City.

2 large onions	1 tablespoon cooking oil
5 stalks spring onion	3 teaspoons soy sauce
1 large carrot	1 teaspoon salt
1/2 pound oyster mushrooms	2 teaspoons sugar
12 ounces dried sweet potato starch noodles	2 teaspoons sesame oil
	2 teaspoons ground sesame seeds

Slice the onions, spring onions, carrot, and mushrooms into long thin shreds.

Bring water to a boil in a large saucepan. Cook the sweet potato noodles for about 2 minutes, or until noodles are soft. Drain the noodles and wash with lukewarm water.

Sauté the sliced vegetables and onions slightly with cooking oil in a frying pan for about 3-4 minutes.

Mix the sautéed vegetables and noodles with the soy sauce, salt, sugar, sesame oil, and sesame seeds in a large bowl, lifting the noodles high in the air.

Per serving: 285 calories; 11 g protein; 54 g carbohydrate; 5 g fat; 5 g fiber; 58 mg calcium; 1029 mg sodium; calories from protein: 14%; calories from carbohydrates: 72%; calories from fats: 14%

PANCHRANGI SABZI

The Taj Mahal Hotel, Lucknow, India

SERVES 4-6

*S*ubstituting soy creamer for dairy cream retains the flavor and increases the health value of this colorful spinach dish.

2 cups frozen chopped spinach, or 1 bunch fresh, cleaned and destemmed
1/4 cup water
2 large mushrooms, diced
1/2 cup grated carrot
1 cup diced cauliflower
1 cup diced green beans
1 cup frozen green peas
8 ounces firm tofu (1/2 block), crumbled

1 tablespoon ~~vegetable oil~~ *broth*
1 teaspoon cumin seed
1 teaspoon grated fresh ginger
2 cloves garlic, minced or pressed
red chili powder to taste
garam masala to taste
salt to taste
1/2 cup plain soy creamer

Boil the spinach in 1/4 cup of water until soft. Mash with a fork or in a food processor to make a paste and set aside.

In a medium saucepan, boil the mushrooms, carrots, cauliflower, and green beans until just soft. Add the peas and crumbled tofu. Remove from heat and set aside.

In a large pot, heat the ~~oil~~ *broth* and add the cumin seeds, ginger, and garlic and cook for 20-30 seconds. Add the tofu and vegetable mixture and heat through, 6-8 minutes.

Add the spinach purée, cook, and stir for 5 more minutes until the mixture is well blended. Add the red chili powder, garam masala, and salt to taste, and stir in the soy creamer to finish.

Per serving: 120 calories; 8 g protein; 12 g carbohydrate; 5 g fat; 4 g fiber; 195 mg calcium; 97 mg sodium; calories from protein: 25%; calories from carbohydrates: 39%; calories from fats: 36%

Vegetables and Grains

GEMÜSEROSTI

Rotes Gatter, Hotel des Balances, Luzern, Switzerland

MAKES 6 PATTIES

*R*osti is a traditional potato dish, similar to hash browns, but served in more generous portions and mixed, if you like, with onions, peppers, mushrooms, and more. To cut the fat in the Swiss original, tofu and mock bacon bits easily replace the usual egg and bacon.

2 medium potatoes	2 tablespoons mock bacon bits,
1 large carrot, shredded and steamed	such as Baco® bits
1/4 onion, minced	salt to taste
2 ounces firm tofu, crumbled	

Place the potatoes in a medium saucepan. Add enough water to cover the potatoes. Bring water to a boil, reduce heat, and simmer for approximately 45 minutes, or until potatoes are easily pierced with a fork. Drain water and allow potatoes to cool. Once cooled, peel and grate them.

In a medium bowl, mix together the grated potatoes, carrot, onion, tofu, and mock bacon bits. Shape into large patties, about 1/4-inch thick. Add salt to taste.

Heat a large, non-stick skillet. Spray liberally with cooking spray. Add the patties and cook about 3 minutes on each side, or until golden brown. Serve warm.

Per serving: 74 calories; 3 g protein; 14 g carbohydrate; 1 g fat; 1.5 g fiber; 23 mg calcium; 49 mg sodium; calories from protein: 15%; calories from carbohydrates: 73%; calories from fats: 12%

SPINACH AND SWEET CORN PORRIDGE

Hangawi Restaurant, New York, New York

SERVES 8

kernels from 2 ears of corn, or about
   1-1/2 cups frozen corn kernels,
   thawed
8-1/2 ounces spinach
2 cups water

1 teaspoon sesame oil *vinegar?*
1 cup chopped onion
1 garlic clove, minced
3/4 cup short-grain white rice
1/2 teaspoon salt

Grind the corn and spinach with 2 cups of water in a blender or food processor until smooth. Next, heat the oil in a saucepan over medium-high heat. Add the onion and garlic. Sauté until onions are soft and translucent. Reduce heat to low. Add the spinach and corn mixture to the saucepan. Stir until blended. Add the rice, stirring until well-blended. Turn heat to high and bring the mixture to a boil. Once boiling, return heat to low. Cover pot and simmer for 20 minutes, stirring occasionally, until rice is soft and mixture is thick. Add salt and mix.

Per serving: 110 calories; 3 g protein; 23 g carbohydrate; 1 g fat; 4 g fiber; 29 mg calcium; 181 mg sodium; calories from protein: 11%; calories from carbohydrates: 82%; calories from fats: 7%

WILD RICE CONFETTI

Gundel Restaurant, Budapest, Hungary

SERVES 4

1 quart water
1 cup wild rice
1 teaspoon salt   *broth*
3 tablespoons vegetable oil
1/2 leek, diced

2 mushrooms, diced
1/2 cup mixed green, red, and
   yellow bell peppers, diced
2 tablespoons chopped fresh parsley
salt and freshly ground white pepper

In a 2-quart saucepan, bring 1 quart of water to a boil. Add the rice and salt and simmer for about 40 minutes, or until the rice is tender. Drain.

In a 10-inch frying pan, heat the oil *broth* over medium-high heat. Sauté the leek for about 2 minutes until golden brown. Add the mushroom, peppers, and parsley, and season to taste with salt and pepper. Sauté for 4-5 minutes. Add the rice and mix well. Serve warm.

Per serving: 247 calories; 6.5 g protein; 32.5 g carbohydrate; 10.5 g fat; 3 g fiber; 17 mg calcium; 587 mg sodium; calories from protein: 10%; calories from carbohydrates: 52%; calories from fats: 38%

BOREK WITH VEGETABLES OR PHYLLO SQUARES WITH A MIXED VEGETABLE CENTER

Mason-Girardot Alan Manor, Windsor, Ontario, Canada

SERVES 10

This old manor house was turned into a gourmet restaurant, with the family feeling still very much in evidence. *Borek* is a Turkish word for a whole family of foods made with thin sheets of pastry such as phyllo dough.

FILLING

2 tablespoons canola oil or other
   vegetable oil
1 jalapeño pepper, or 1 whole, dried
   red chili
2 cups finely chopped onions
1 teaspoon minced garlic
2 pounds mixed vegetables
   (zucchini, peas, carrots, sweet
   corn, potatoes), finely diced

1 tablespoon coriander powder
1/2 tablespoon cumin powder
1/2 cup lemon juice
salt to taste
1/2 cup water

PHYLLO

1/2 pound vegan phyllo pastry
   (available from most Greek, Turkish,
   Indian, or Middle Eastern grocers)

3 tablespoons olive oil
1 cup soymilk

Note: The filling can be prepared ahead of time and held in the refrigerator.

For the filling: Heat the oil in a frying pan until very hot. Add the jalapeño. The heat will pop the jalapeño and infuse its flavor into the oil. Remove immediately. (Failure to remove the pepper immediately will lead to the jalapeño overwhelming the flavor of vegetables and ruin later enjoyment.) Turn the heat to low. Add the chopped onions and sauté until soft, but not brown, to impart a natural sweetness to offset the spice in the dish. Add the minced garlic. Sauté for 30-40 seconds. Add the mixed vegetables and stir gently. Continue to stir occasionally to make sure the vegetables do not stick to the pan. If the vegetables do stick, add a few drops of water at a time to release the vegetables. Add the coriander and cumin powders and fold in the spices to coat the vegetable mixture evenly. Add the lemon juice and salt. Add a little water, cover the pan, and cook gently for another 3 minutes or so until vegetables are partly cooked, firm to the bite. You do not want to cook them fully as this will happen in the baking process. The mixture should be moist, but not watery.

For the phyllo: Preheat oven to 350°F. Mix the soymilk and olive oil in a cup. With a pastry brush, brush the base of a 9- by 12-inch baking pan with the soymilk and olive oil mixture.

Work with one layer of the dough at a time. Line the brushed baking tray with one sheet of phyllo dough. Brush the dough with the soymilk/olive oil mixture. Work in quick succession, layering up to 5 or 6 sheets and brushing each with the soymilk/olive oil mixture.

Spread the vegetable filling evenly over the pastry. Layer with another 5-6 sheets of pastry successively brushed with the soymilk/olive oil mixture. You'll now have a tray full of vegetable mixture sandwiched between 2 layers of brushed pastry.

Make horizontal cuts in the tray, slicing through to the bottom. Next, make vertical cuts, slicing through to the bottom. You now have the borek divided in small squares. Cutting ahead of time like this will help in lifting off the squares once the borek is baked.

Place the tray in the oven and bake 30-40 minutes until the borek is puffed up and golden brown. Serve hot or cold with your sauce or salsa of choice.

Per serving: 205 calories; 5 g protein; 28 g carbohydrate; 9 g fat; 4 g fiber; 27 mg calcium; 161 mg sodium; calories from protein: 9%; calories from carbohydrates: 53%; calories from fats: 38%

POLENTA

Crackers, Norfolk, Virginia

SERVES 12

*T*his tiny, friendly tapas restaurant specializes in delicate dishes, including this savory polenta, which goes well with blackened asparagus and a spicy chickpea dip on grilled pita bread.

1 quart soymilk	1/4 teaspoon cayenne pepper
3 cups water	1 teaspoon dried basil
1 teaspoon salt	2-1/2 cups cornmeal
1/2 teaspoon black pepper	1-1/2 cups black beans

Preheat oven to 500°F.

Bring soymilk and water to a boil and then reduce to a simmer. Season with the salt, black pepper, cayenne pepper, and dried basil. Add the cornmeal slowly, while stirring, until it's the consistency of porridge and does not stick to the sides of the pan. Stir in the black beans. Pour the mixture into a 12- by 8-inch greased pan and bake at 500°F for 18-20 minutes.

Per serving: 80 calories; 5 g protein; 12 g carbohydrate; 2 g fat; 3 g fiber; 10 mg calcium; 204 mg sodium; calories from protein: 23%; calories from carbohydrates: 58%; calories from fats: 19%

SPICY KIMCHI MUSHROOM PANCAKES

Hangawi, New York, New York

MAKES 10 LARGE PANCAKES

*K*imchi is a staple on Korean dinner tables. This spicy, seasoned pickled cabbage is available at Asian markets and many specialty grocers and health food stores.

2 pounds (2 15- or 16-ounce jars) kimchi	1-1/2 cups water
1/2 pound oyster mushrooms	1 tablespoon minced garlic
4 stalks spring onions	2 teaspoons salt
1 pound wheat flour	3 teaspoons vegetable oil

Drain the kimchi and then dice it along with the oyster mushrooms and spring onions.

In a large bowl, mix the flour with the water, garlic, and salt until the batter is evenly blended. Add the kimchi, spring onions, and mushrooms to the batter and mix well.

Scoop a full ladle of the batter and fry the pancake in a heated skillet with vegetable oil, making sure that both sides are cooked evenly until light brown.

The pancakes should be about 5 inches in diameter.

Per serving: 205 calories; 7 g protein; 40 g carbohydrate; 2 g fat; 5 g fiber; 86 mg calcium; 482 mg sodium; calories from protein: 14%; calories from carbohydrates: 77%; calories from fats: 9%

MASHED POTATOES WITH ONION

Gundel Restaurant, Budapest, Hungary

SERVES 4

4 medium red potatoes, with peels
2 tablespoons vegetable oil
2 onions, finely chopped
salt and freshly ground white pepper
  to taste

rosemary, oregano, or crushed red
  pepper for added flavor (optional)
1 tablespoon dried breadcrumbs

Cook the potatoes in salted boiling water for 15-20 minutes until tender. Drain and let cool for about 5 minutes. Using a potato masher or fork, mash the potatoes (do not purée them).

In a frying pan, heat 1 tablespoon of the oil over medium-high heat. Add the onions and sauté until golden brown. Mix the onions into the potatoes and season to taste with salt, pepper, and any optional herbs and spices.

Heat the remaining tablespoon of oil in a nonstick frying pan over medium heat. Spread the breadcrumbs in the pan and spoon the mashed potatoes over them. Press the potatoes into the pan to cover the breadcrumbs and cook for 8 minutes without turning. Invert the potato cake onto a plate and then return it to the pan with the uncooked side down. Cook for about 8 minutes longer, until both sides are browned. Cut into 4 slices and serve hot.

Per serving: 191 calories; 3 g protein; 30 g carbohydrate; 7 g fat; 3 g fiber; 17 mg calcium; 10 mg sodium; calories from protein: 6%; calories from carbohydrates: 62%; calories from fats: 32%

Desserts

LEMON MARGARITA CAKE WITH TEQUILA ICING

The Taphouse Grill, Norfolk, Virginia

SERVES 8

A sunburst painting greets you as you decide whether to sit on the quiet, outdoor patio or the smoky, indoor area featuring a band (from punk to country). Enjoy a vast international beer menu and the chef's daily vegan specials.

CAKE

Egg Replacer,® enough to equal 2 eggs	1/2 teaspoon salt
1/2 cup vegetable oil	1/4 cup lime juice from 4 large limes
1 cup sugar	zest of 4 limes, minced
1-1/4 cup all-purpose flour	1 teaspoon vanilla extract
2 teaspoons baking powder	

Preheat oven to 350°F.

Follow directions for preparing the Egg Replacer.® In a large bowl, beat the vegetable oil into the Egg Replacer.® Then, slowly beat in the sugar.

In a separate bowl, combine the flour, baking powder, and salt. Fold the flour mixture into the blended mixture. Do not over fold, but make sure there are no pockets of flour in the batter. Blend in the lime juice, lime zest, and vanilla. Pour the batter into a 12-inch round pan that has been lightly greased and floured, or has a parchment paper-lined bottom.

Bake 25-30 minutes at 350°F, or until lightly brown and a tooth-pick comes out clean. Let cool and remove the cake pan.

TEQUILA ICING

1/4 cup softened soy margarine
1-1/2 cups icing sugar

1 teaspoon vanilla extract
1 tablespoon tequila

For the icing: With a hand mixer, blend the soy margarine. Add the sugar and vanilla. Slowly add the tequila and blend until smooth.

Ice the cooled cake and garnish with lime slices.

Per serving: 485 calories; 2 g protein; 77 g carbohydrate; 19 g fat; 1 g fiber; 56 mg calcium; 313 mg sodium; calories from protein: 2%; calories from carbohydrates: 62%; calories from fats: 35%; calories from alcohol: 1%

ROSEMARY-GRAPEFRUIT SORBET

TJ's Restaurant and Lounge, Richmond, Virginia

MAKES 1 QUART

*Y*ou'll need an ice cream maker for this delightful dessert.

1 cup water
1 cup sugar
2 teaspoons fresh, whole rosemary
  leaves

3 cups red grapefruit juice
1 tablespoon lemon juice
2 tablespoons lime juice

In a small saucepan, bring the water and sugar to a boil. Reduce the heat to medium and simmer the mixture until all the sugar is dissolved. Remove the pan from the heat.

Lightly bruise* the rosemary leaves, but do not cut. Add the rosemary to the sugar mixture and allow to cool to room temperature.

Remove the rosemary leaves and discard. Add the remaining juices to the sugar mixture and process in the can of an ice cream freezer according to the manufacturer's instructions.

* *To bruise the rosemary leaves, squeeze them with a mortar and pestle.*

Per serving: 261 calories; 1 g protein; 66 g carbohydrate; 0 g fat; 0 g fiber; 18 mg calcium; 2 mg sodium; calories from protein: 1%; calories from carbohydrates: 98%; calories from fats: 1%

BUTTERSCOTCH MOUSSE

O_2, Los Angeles, California

SERVES 6

*S*weetened with nutrient-rich dates rather than sugar, this creamy dessert makes a healthy finish to a meal.

1 cup raw cashews	1/8 teaspoon nutmeg
1 cup soft, pitted dates (packed measure)	1/2 teaspoon cinnamon
	1/2 teaspoon butterscotch extract
1 cup water	6 kiwis, sliced

In a food processor, grind the cashews for approximately 2 minutes until the consistency of ground meal. Add the dates and process 1 minute, or until you reach a pasty consistency. Gradually add the water and blend until smooth and creamy. Add the nutmeg, cinnamon, and butterscotch extract. Process a couple more seconds until completely blended. Serve in chilled glasses layered with slices of kiwi.

Per serving: 259 calories; 5 g protein; 39 g carbohydrate; 10 g fat; 5 g fiber; 40 mg calcium; 8 mg sodium; calories from protein: 6%; calories from carbohydrates: 60%; calories from fats: 34%

ICED HONEYDEW SOUP WITH TOKAJI WINE

Gundel Restaurant, Budapest, Hungary

SERVES 4

A refreshing Hungarian treat.

1 honeydew melon (about 4 pounds)	1/2 cup semi-sweet white wine
3 tablespoons Tokaji Aszú or other sweet dessert wine of your choice	3 tablespoons plain soy creamer
	1 bunch fresh mint (garnish)

Cut off the top of the melon with a zig-zag cut. Remove the seeds with a spoon.

Cut 16 balls from the melon with a melon-baller. Put the balls into a cup, add the sweet dessert wine, and refrigerate.

Scrape the remaining melon flesh into a 4-quart bowl. Refrigerate the melon rind intact. Add the white wine and soy creamer to the melon flesh, cover, and refrigerate until chilled.

Purée the chilled melon in a blender or food processor and re-frigerate the soup for at least 1 hour.

Pour the refrigerated soup into the chilled rind. Add the melon balls and the sweet dessert wine accumulated in the cup into the soup. Present the soup in the rind on the table, garnished with fresh mint. Serve in chilled cups.

Per serving: 204 calories; 2 g protein; 45 g carbohydrate; 1 g fat; 3 g fiber; 31 mg calcium; 55 mg sodium; calories from protein: 3%; calories from carbohydrates: 83%; calories from fats: 2%; calories from alcohol: 12%

GRATIN DE POMMES AU CALVADOS

La Bretonnière, Grimaud, France

SERVES 4

Calvados is an apple brandy popular in Normandy, often said to aid digestion. We used vanilla soy yogurt instead of cream to trim the fat content, but not the flavor.

vegetable oil cooking spray
4 tart cooking apples, peeled, cored, and thinly sliced
juice of 1/2 lemon
2 tablespoons calvados (apple-flavored brandy)

1/2 cup apple juice
1/2 cup brown sugar
1 teaspoon ground cinnamon
1/2 cup vanilla soy yogurt

Preheat oven to 400°F.

Spray the bottom of a 9- by 12-inch baking pan with oil. Layer the bottom of the pan evenly with the apple slices. Sprinkle with the lemon juice, calvados, apple juice, brown sugar, and cinnamon.

Bake until the fruit edges are tinged with dark brown, about 25 minutes.

Serve immediately with a dollop of vanilla soy yogurt.

Per serving: 207 calories; 1 g protein; 48 g carbohydrate; 1 g fat; 4 g fiber; 30 mg calcium; 14 mg sodium; calories from protein: 1%; calories from carbohydrates: 90%; calories from fats: 3%; calories from alcohol: 6%

LA TARTE AUX FIGUES

Restaurant Le Rive Droite, Nice, France

SERVES 8

TART CRUST

1 cup all-purpose flour	1 tablespoon powdered sugar
4 tablespoons ice water	1 ounce non-dairy cream cheese
1/2 teaspoon vinegar	1/4 cup vegetable shortening

TART FILLING

4 ounces non-dairy cream cheese	1/3 cup orange juice
1/8 cup sugar	1/4 cup raspberry jam
16 ounces fresh black mission figs, cut into disks or circles	1 tablespoon sugar
	1 tablespoon cornstarch

For the crust: Preheat oven to 400°F. In a small bowl, whisk together 1/4 cup of the flour with the ice water and vinegar. In a separate bowl, combine the remaining 3/4 cup of flour with the sugar. Cut in the non-dairy cream cheese and shortening with a fork or a pastry cutter until the mixture resembles crumbs. Add other flour mixture, stirring until the mixture is moist. Shape the dough into a small ball and place on a sheet of waxed paper. Place another sheet on top and roll out the dough to form a 12-inch disk. Place the dough in the freezer for 15 minutes.

After removing dough from freezer, peel off the top sheet of waxed paper. Place a 9-inch pie or tart pan already coated with cooking spray, upside down on top of dough disk. Flip the dish and dough so the dough is now on top with the waxed paper-side facing upward. Remove the waved paper and press the dough into the dish. Press the edges of the dough with a fork. Fill the dough with pie weights or dried beans to weigh it down. Place in the oven and bake for 20 minutes, or until golden brown. Remove and cool on a wire rack.

For the filling: Using a mixer, blend the non-dairy cream cheese and sugar in a bowl. Spread onto the bottom of the cooled crust. Top with fig circles. Meanwhile, combine the remaining ingredients (orange juice through cornstarch) in a small saucepan. Heat over medium heat until thickened. Pour over the figs. Put the tart in the refrigerator until serving.

Per serving: 257 calories; 3 g protein; 37 g carbohydrate; 12 g fat; 2.5 g fiber; 25 mg calcium; 89 mg sodium; calories from protein: 4%; calories from carbohydrates: 57%; calories from fats: 39%

GEZOGENER APFELSTRUDEL

Griechenbeisl, Vienna, Austria

SERVES 8

*A*t Griechenbeisl, the strudel dough is hand-pulled. However, using phyllo dough lets you make this Austrian treat in half the time. For variety, use other fruits such as pears, apricots, or plums instead of apples.

2-1/2 pounds slightly sour, peeled
    apples with seeds removed
1/4 cup soft soy margarine, plus
    enough to spread over the dough
3/4 cup breadcrumbs
3/4 cup crystal sugar or rock sugar
2 teaspoons vanilla extract

1 teaspoon cinnamon
2 tablespoons rum
1/2 cup raisins
1 pound vegan phyllo dough
powdered sugar to sprinkle over
    baked strudel

Preheat oven to 400°F.

Cut the apples into quarters, then into 1/8-inch slices. Heat the soy margarine in a pan, then add the breadcrumbs and roast until golden brown. Let cool.

Mix the apples with the sugar, vanilla, cinnamon, rum, and raisins.

Spread the soy margarine evenly over the phyllo dough and layer the breadcrumbs on top, followed by the apple mixture, leaving a 1/2-inch margin on all sides. Roll the strudel tightly and close the ends. Place on a greased baking sheet. Spread more soy margarine over the top of the strudel. Bake for about 40 minutes.

Sprinkle with powdered sugar. Slice into 8 pieces. Serve hot or cold.

Per serving: 414 calories; 5 g protein; 79 g carbohydrate; 10 g fat; 5 g fiber; 27 mg calcium; 359 mg sodium; calories from protein: 5%; calories from carbohydrates: 75%; calories from fats: 20%

SOUPE A L'ORANGE

Tabou Plage, Saint-Tropez, France

SERVES 4

*A*s close to Heaven as you could ever want to be, your waiter will bring lunch while you gaze from your shaded chair over *le Grand Bleu* towards Brigitte Bardot's home. This dessert is little more than a wisp of sweetness.

1-1/2 cups water
1 cup sugar
5 oranges
1/2 cup fresh mint leaves

splash of Grand Marnier, or 1/8
teaspoon orange extract
2 cups chopped strawberries

Combine the water and sugar. Bring the mixture to a brief boil and then allow to cool.

Cut the oranges into slices and remove their white inner tissues. Finely slice the mint leaves, discarding stems. Mix together the sugar-water mixture, orange slices, and mint. Let stand for 2-3 hours.

Add a splash of Grand Marnier or orange extract and the chopped strawberries right before serving.

Per serving: 287 calories; 2 g protein; 73 g carbohydrate; 0.5 g fat; 6 g fiber; 84 mg calcium; 2 mg sodium; calories from protein: 2%; calories from carbohydrates: 96%; calories from fats: 2%

TOFU CUSTARD

Health Haven, Toronto, Canada

SERVES 5

1 pound silken or soft tofu
2 teaspoons vanilla extract
2 teaspoons vanilla custard powder

5 teaspoons maple syrup
5 mint sprigs (garnish)

Pressing the tofu: Slice the tofu into uniformly thick slices. Place two layers of paper towel onto a cookie sheet. Place the tofu slices on top of the paper towels and then put another two layers of paper towel on top of the tofu. Cover with plastic wrap and then place approximately a 5-pound weight on top. (Or, place another cookie sheet on top of the tofu and then place a 5-pound weight on top of the cookie sheet.) Let sit for 1 hour.

Preheat oven to 375°F.

In a blender or food processor, blend the pressed tofu, vanilla, and vanilla custard powder until smooth and creamy.

Place 1 teaspoon of maple syrup on the bottoms of 5 greased or nonstick muffin tins. Spoon in the blended tofu mixture. Place the muffin tin on a baking sheet. Bake for 15-20 minutes, or until the tofu sets and turns slightly golden brown.

Let cool. Invert on individual plates. Garnish with mint sprigs and serve.

Per serving: 76 calories; 6 g protein; 7 g carbohydrate; 3 g fat; 1 g fiber; 34 mg calcium; 33 mg sodium; calories from protein: 31%; calories from carbohydrates: 34%; calories from fats: 30%; calories from alcohol: 5%

Breakfasts

FLAXSEED-APPLE-BATTERED FRENCH TOAST WITH WARM APPLE COMPOTE

Millenium, San Francisco, California

SERVES 4

*F*laxseeds give this morning meal an egg-like consistency without added cholesterol. The compote is a perfect complement and easy to make, too.

BATTER

1 tablespoon flaxseeds
1/2 cup applesauce
2 cups calcium-fortified soymilk
1/2 teaspoon ground nutmeg
1 teaspoon ground cinnamon

1/4 teaspoon sea salt
8 thick slices whole-grain bread,
    stale or air-dried overnight
1/4 cup oil (optional)

WARM APPLE COMPOTE

3 apples, peeled, cored, and cut into
    1/2-inch-thick slices
1 cup apple juice
2 tablespoons maple syrup or Sucanat®
1 teaspoon minced orange zest
1/4 teaspoon ground cloves

1/4 teaspoon ground allspice
1/2 teaspoon ground cinnamon
2 teaspoons minced fresh ginger
1/4 teaspoon ground pepper
1/4 teaspoon sea salt

To make the batter: Combine flaxseeds, applesauce, soymilk, nutmeg, cinnamon, and sea salt in a blender and purée until smooth. Place in a large, shallow bowl. Dip 2 slices of bread at a time into the batter to coat evenly. In a large sauté pan or skillet, cook the bread in the oil over medium heat on both sides until lightly brown. Or, cook the bread in a dry nonstick pan. Repeat with the remaining bread.

For the warm apple compote: In a large, non-reactive* saucepan, combine all the compote ingredients and bring to a boil. Reduce to a simmer and cook until the liquid reduces to a light syrup, about 15 minutes. Serve warm. Store in an airtight container in the refrigerator for up to 4 days.

Serve 2 slices per serving with 1/2 cup of the apple compote.

A non-reactive saucepan is a pan that is not lined with aluminum, which can react with certain ingredients, like acids. All-Clad pans are non-reactive.

Per serving (with oil): 459 calories; 10 g protein; 62 g carbohydrate; 19 g fat; 9 g fiber; 368 mg calcium; 535 mg sodium; calories from protein: 9%; calories from carbohydrates: 55%; calories from fats: 36%

Per serving (without oil): 333 calories; 10 g protein; 62 g carbohydrate; 5 g fat; 9 g fiber; 368 mg calcium; 535 mg sodium; calories from protein: 12%; calories from carbohydrates: 74%; calories from fats: 14%

BANANA CAKE

Taj Mahal, New Delhi, India

MAKES ABOUT 12 PIECES

A top-of-the-line hotel with a top-of-the-line chef, serving delightful international and Indian dishes. This banana cake is so light that it almost floats away. It's perfect served as a breakfast bread.

1/2 cup water
2 very ripe bananas
1/2 cup granulated or breakfast sugar
1/4 cup vegetable oil

1 teaspoon vanilla essence
2 cups flour
1 teaspoon baking soda
1/2 teaspoon salt

Preheat oven to 325°F.

Blend the water, bananas, and sugar until smooth. Gradually add the oil and vanilla, and blend until smooth.

Sift the flour, baking soda, and salt together twice. Combine the flour and blended mixture together, and mix well.

Put the mixture into a greased 9- by 9-inch pan. Bake for about 40 minutes, until the top is golden brown. Let the cake cool before cutting.

Per serving: 165 calories; 2 g protein; 28 g carbohydrate; 5 g fat; 1 g fiber; 4 mg calcium; 202 mg sodium; calories from protein: 6%; calories from carbohydrates: 68%; calories from fats: 26%

GUNDEL-PANCAKE

Hotel Gellert, Budapest, Hungary

MAKES 4 CRÊPES

*C*rêpes can be an appetizer, a main dish, or a fabulous dessert. For chocolate lovers, they can be topped with a fat-free chocolate sauce.

CRÊPES

3/4 cup unbleached white flour
1/2 teaspoon salt
1/2 teaspoon baking powder

1 cup soy creamer
1/4 teaspoon vanilla extract
cooking spray

FILLING

1/2 cup water
1 tablespoon sugar
1/4 cup raisins

1 cup puréed pecans (about 2 cups pecan halves)

TOPPING

warm cinnamon applesauce or maple syrup

For the crêpes: Place the flour, salt, and baking powder in a blender or food processor. Process until blended. Slowly add creamer and vanilla, processing until smooth. Spray a non-stick skillet with cooking spray. Heat over medium heat. Once hot, add about 1/4 cup of the crêpe mixture to the pan, swirling it around so the entire pan is covered with a thin layer of crêpe batter. Once the top of the crêpe is dry and the underside is lightly brown, flip over the crêpe. Cook the other side until lightly browned. Proceed with the remaining batter. Set aside the crêpes, keeping them warm.

For the filling: Add the water and sugar to a saucepan. Bring to a boil. Add the raisins. Lower the heat to medium and add the puréed nuts. Cook the mixture until creamy, adding water as needed. Once the mixture has the consistency of a creamy paste, remove from heat.

Add about 1/4 cup of the filling to the middle of each crêpe. Roll each crêpe and top with applesauce or syrup.

Per serving: 197 calories; 9 g protein; 63 g carbohydrate; 38 g fat; 5 g fiber; 44 mg calcium; 383 mg sodium; calories from protein: 6%; calories from carbohydrates: 39%; calories from fats: 55%

BLATTERTEIG-APFELSTRUDEL

Griechenbeisl, Vienna, Austria

Serves 10

This strudel recipe uses Egg Replacer® instead of whole eggs to make it a cholesterol-free, early morning treat. It is delicious served as a breakfast pastry with herbal tea.

2-1/2 pounds slightly sour, peeled apples with seeds removed (about 3 apples)
1/2 cup crystal sugar or rock sugar
1 teaspoon vanilla extract
1 tablespoon cinnamon
1 tablespoon lemon juice
1 tablespoon rum
1/2 cup raisins

2 tablespoons soy margarine, plus more to spread over the dough
1 pound vegan puff pastry or phyllo dough
Egg Replacer,® enough to equal about 2 eggs
powdered sugar to sprinkle over baked strudel

Preheat oven to 400°F.

Cut the apples into small cubes and mix with the sugar, vanilla, cinnamon, lemon juice, rum, and raisins. Melt the soy margarine in a medium saucepan and then add the apples. Let cool.

Roll out the puff pastry to approximately 9- by 12-inches. Or, if using phyllo dough, layer 3 sheets on top of one another, spreading soy margarine on each sheet. Cut off two 1-inch strips lengthwise. Set aside. Place the dough on a greased baking sheet. Put the cooked apples on 1/2 of the dough. Coat the dough with Egg Replacer.® Fold the dough in half, covering the apples. Press the sides together. Spread more Egg Replacer® over the top of the strudel. Use the dough strips to decorate the top of the strudel by making "s"-shaped waves with the dough. Coat the strips with Egg Replacer.®

Bake for about 25 minutes. Sprinkle with powdered sugar. Slice into 10 pieces and serve warm.

Per serving: 256 calories; 4 g protein; 47 g carbohydrate; 6 g fat; 2 g fiber; 39 mg calcium; 261 mg sodium; calories from protein: 6%; calories from carbohydrates: 73%; calories from fats: 21%

Millennium Oat and Walnut Pancakes with Blueberry-Orange Sauce

Millenium, San Francisco, California

SERVES 4

*W*alnuts give these multigrain pancakes a delightful texture and flavor. A great weekend staple with this quick blueberry-orange sauce.

PANCAKES

1 cup unbleached all-purpose flour
1/2 cup whole-wheat flour
1/2 cup corn flour
1/3 cup walnuts, toasted and crushed in a plastic bag with a rolling pin
1/4 cup rolled oats
2 teaspoons Sucanat® or unrefined sugar (optional)

1/4 teaspoon ground allspice
1/2 teaspoon ground cinnamon
1/4 teaspoon sea salt
1 teaspoon baking powder
3 cups calcium-fortified soymilk or rice milk
1 teaspoon champagne vinegar or rice vinegar

BLUEBERRY-ORANGE SAUCE

2 cups fresh or frozen blueberries
1/2 cup apple juice
1/2 cup fresh orange juice
1 teaspoon orange zest, minced

1 tablespoon Sucanat® or unrefined sugar
1 teaspoon fresh ginger, minced

For the pancakes: In a large bowl, mix the flours, walnuts, oats, Sucanat,® allspice, cinnamon, salt, and baking powder together well. In a medium bowl, mix the soymilk and vinegar together. Add the liquid ingredients to the dry ingredients and whisk until well incorporated. The resulting batter should be a little thicker than heavy cream. Pour 1/2 cup of batter per pancake onto a lightly oiled, nonstick sauté pan or skillet and cook until lightly browned on each side. Serve with blueberry-orange sauce.

For the sauce: Place all the ingredients in a non-reactive* saucepan. Cook over medium heat, stirring occasionally, for 15 minutes, or until the blueberries are soft and the remaining liquid is syrupy. Serve warm.

* *A non-reactive saucepan is a pan that is not lined with aluminum, which can*

react with certain ingredients, like acids. All-Clad pans are non-reactive.

Per serving (with 1/4-cup sauce): 419 calories; 14 g protein; 66 g carbohydrate; 11 g fat; 9 g fiber; 260 mg calcium; 307 mg sodium; calories from protein: 13%; calories from carbohydrates: 63%; calories from fats: 24%

(ANY TIME)

SOUTHWEST BREAKFAST BURRITO

The Painted Table, Seattle, Washington

SERVES 2

1 tablespoon oil *broth*	1 teaspoon vinegar
1 cup chopped onion	1 9-ounce can diced tomatoes
2 teaspoons minced garlic	1 chipotle pepper, dried
2 teaspoons ground cumin	1/4 cup diced bell pepper
2 teaspoons ground coriander	1 pound extra-firm tofu, crumbled *pressed*
1 9-ounce can black beans, drained and rinsed	1-1/2 cups vegan soy cheese (cheddar flavor)
1/4 cup water	4 small flour tortillas

For the beans: In a medium skillet, heat 1 teaspoon of olive *broth* oil. Add 4 tablespoons of the chopped onion and sauté until tender. Add the garlic, cumin, and coriander and then cook 1 minute more. Add the black beans and 1/4 cup of water. Simmer until most of the liquid has evaporated. Stir in the vinegar and half of the tomatoes. Set aside and keep warm.

For the sauce: Soak the chipotle in warm water until soft. Discard the water, cut off the top stem, and remove the seeds. In a small mixing bowl, add the chipotle and the other half of the diced tomatoes. Purée until smooth. Set aside.

For the tortilla filling: In a medium skillet, heat 2 teaspoons of olive *broth* oil. Add the bell pepper and remaining onion and sauté until tender. Add the crumbled tofu and cook until thoroughly heated.

To assemble: Warm the flour tortillas. Divide the tofu mixture amongst the tortillas. Top with soy cheese and roll. Top the tortillas with tomato sauce. Serve with beans on the side.

Per serving: 751 calories; 58 g protein; 82 g carbohydrate; 37 g fat; 15 g fiber; 888 mg calcium; 1433 mg sodium; calories from protein: 26%; calories from carbohydrates: 37%; calories from fats: 37%

THE BENEDICT

Millennium, San Francisco, California

SERVES 4

This healthy version of eggs Benedict uses a delicious blend of vegetables and smoked tofu for a low-fat but hearty way to start the day.

GRILLED ONIONS AND TOMATOES

1/4 cup fresh orange juice
1 clove garlic, minced
1/2 teaspoon sea salt
1 large red onion, cut into 1/3-inch
   slices

2 tomatoes, halved crosswise
2 teaspoons olive oil *broth or spray*

SAUTÉED SPINACH

2 teaspoons olive oil *broth*
1 clove garlic, minced
4 cups packed spinach leaves
sea salt to taste
12 ounces smoked tofu, cut
   lengthwise into 4 slices
1 teaspoon canola oil *broth*

4 slices toasted focaccia or English
   muffin halves
Citrus Béarnaise-Style Sauce (recipe
   follows)
chopped fresh parsley or chives
   (garnish)

To make the grilled vegetables: Preheat the broiler. In a shallow bowl, combine the orange juice, garlic, salt, onion, tomatoes, and ~~oil.~~ Let set for 10 minutes. Broil the onions and tomato halves until the onions are slightly soft and browned, about 10 minutes. Set aside.

To make the spinach: In a medium sauté pan or skillet, sauté the garlic in the ~~oil~~ *broth* over medium heat until lightly browned. Remove from heat and add the spinach. Toss the spinach until just wilted. Add salt to taste and set aside.

Brush the tofu slices with the ~~canola oil~~ *broth.* Broil for 2 minutes, or until the top is lightly browned and blistered, or, if you prefer, grill the tofu for 1-2 minutes on each side.

For each serving, place a focaccia slice in the center of a plate. Top with a slice of tofu, a portion of wilted spinach, slices of grilled onion, and a grilled tomato half. Ladle over 1/3 cup of sauce and garnish with the chopped herbs. Serve immediately.

CITRUS BÉARNAISE-STYLE SAUCE

4 shallots
2/3 cup dry white wine or nonalcoholic white wine
2 tablespoons champagne vinegar
2 teaspoons minced fresh thyme
1/2 teaspoon dried sage
1 tablespoon minced fresh tarragon
1/2 teaspoon ground pepper
1/4 teaspoon saffron threads
1/2 teaspoon minced lemon zest

1/2 teaspoon minced orange zest
1/4 cup fresh lemon juice
1/4 cup fresh orange juice
2 teaspoons nutritional yeast
1/2 cup Cashew Cream (recipe follows)
1/2 cup calcium-fortified rice milk or soymilk
sea salt to taste

In a medium, non-reactive* saucepan, bring the shallots, wine, and vinegar to a boil over medium heat. Cook to reduce by half, then add the thyme, sage, tarragon, pepper, saffron, zests, and juices. Cook to reduce by half again. Remove from heat and stir in the yeast, cashew cream, and rice milk. Add salt, if desired. Serve warm or store in an airtight container in the refrigerator for up to 4 days. Reheat to serve.

CASHEW CREAM

1/2 cup unsalted cashews

1 cup water, plus more as needed

In a blender, combine the cashews and 1/2 cup of water. Blend until coarsely puréed. Slowly add the remaining 1/2 cup of water until smooth. Add additional water if needed to thin to the consistency of heavy cream. Store refrigerated in an airtight container for up to 4 days.

A non-reactive saucepan is a pan that is not lined with aluminum, which can react with certain ingredients, like acids. All-Clad pans are non-reactive.

Per serving: 313 calories; 17 g protein; 41 g carbohydrate; 9 g fat; 6 g fiber; 260 mg calcium; 675 mg sodium; calories from protein: 22%; calories from carbohydrates: 52%; calories from fats: 26%